What Teachers Expect in Reform

Making Their Voices Heard

Penny Ann Armstrong

Rowman & Littlefield Education
Lanham, Maryland • Toronto • Plymouth, UK
2008

Published in the United States of America
by Rowman & Littlefield Education
A Division of Rowman & Littlefield Publishers, Inc.
A wholly owned subsidiary of The Rowman & Littlefield Publishing Group, Inc.
4501 Forbes Boulevard, Suite 200, Lanham, Maryland 20706
www.rowmaneducation.com

Estover Road
Plymouth PL6 7PY
United Kingdom

British Library Cataloguing in Publication Information Available

Library of Congress Cataloging-in-Publication Data

Armstrong, Penny Ann, 1951–
  What teachers expect in reform : making their voices heard / Penny Ann
Armstrong.
      p. cm.
  Includes bibliographical references.
  ISBN-13: 978-1-57886-719-6 (hardcover : alk. paper)
  ISBN-13: 978-1-57886-720-2 (pbk. : alk. paper)
  ISBN-10: 1-57886-719-3 (hardcover : alk. paper)
  ISBN-10: 1-57886-720-7 (pbk. : alk. paper)
  1. Educational change—United States. 2. Educational accountability—United
States. 3. Education and state—United States. I. Title.

  LA210.A777 2008
  370.973—dc22   2007032570

⊗™ The paper used in this publication meets the minimum requirements of
American National Standard for Information Sciences—Permanence of Paper
for Printed Library Materials, ANSI/NISO Z39.48-1992.
Manufactured in the United States of America.

To Anna Gallagher, who lit the path for the rest of us.

I look at us as a profession and I think, we know better
than anybody what's going on with this profession and we
know who is doing a good job and who is not doing a good job
and who has the skills and who drags things down and all that.
But somewhere in here, I don't see us talking about it.
I don't see us expressing this. There's this wall of silence.
And these raging voices from the outside telling us what's
wrong and what's not wrong . . . and we are silent.

—classroom teacher

Contents

Reader's Note

This study includes the observations and conclusions of more than 300 educators from Minnesota, New Hampshire, and Texas. The topics are controversial, and the responses are often passionate. During the course of the interviews, educators expressed concerns about consequences if they were identified as not being supportive of district decisions or state education agencies' mandates. Their reluctance to be identified was further indication of the strain they feel in their profession. To protect their identities, I established a record-keeping system that provides accurate reference without directly naming the person being quoted. I organized interviews through a coding system that identified the person, school, and date. Those reference numbers follow each quote. I also identified the position of the person being quoted to provide additional insight and perspective. This book is the culmination of many hours of honest and frank reflection on the part of our teachers.

I

THE HISTORY AND EVOLUTION OF EDUCATION REFORM

1

Education Reform: Classroom Teachers
on the Outside Looking In

Education policy has captured the imagination of the American people. One can hardly pick up a newspaper without reading something about local test scores, beleaguered superintendents, or budget battles between school boards and teachers' unions. Federal improvement plans have become touted education platforms in national political campaigns and government officials have declared stiff penalties for schools that can't "make the grade." Through all of this, classroom teachers have been identified as the responsible party and focus of improved performance. This study presents the teachers' perspective on those conclusions.

Classroom teachers have always operated in a highly complex and dynamic system of procedures, philosophies, and political agendas. What they teach, how they teach, when they teach, and to whom have historically shifted as political thought, economic conditions, and the perceived needs of the country have responded to external and internal events. While reinvention and redefinition have always been part of education, the national call for reform launched in the 1980s was unique in its globally driven economic agenda and its focus on the work of teachers (Apple, 1990; Cohn & Kottkamp, 1993; Kirst, 1987; Mitchell & Encarnation, 1984; Tyack, 1990).

The No Child Left Behind Act (NCLB) (2002) is the centerpiece of President George W. Bush's education reform platform. It was conceived in the early 1980s. The country was facing an economic crisis. Federally appointed commissions on education and leaders in the business community identified schools as being responsible for this turbulence. The consensus was that classroom teachers were not adequately preparing students to compete in the global market and the nation was "at risk" if changes in the work of teachers were not instituted. The reform advocates included the National Commission on Excellence in Education (1983), the Carnegie Forum on Education and the Economy (1986), the Holmes Group (1986), the Education Commission of the States (1983), and the National Governor's Association (1986). These commissions and business leaders recommended a new national education effort to change the goals of public education and take control of classroom teachers. A new way of looking at education was set into motion that would lead to an economically defined agenda in curriculum focus and a high-stakes framework of accountability for classroom teachers.

THE CREATION OF A STUDY

I worked as an assistant principal in a school district in Minnesota from 1996 to 1998. I was directly involved in the implementation of the Goals 2000: Educate America Act (1994) in our district. I worked in a building of strong, committed teachers who were established veterans in the profession. I watched a change come over them as they worked through the newly established state and federal guidelines. Fundamental elements of teaching were being drastically revised and it occurred to me that these teachers had not had a voice in defining what was "wrong" with what they had been doing or in deciding what needed to be done to fix the "problems." As we worked through the early curriculum meetings, they commented on elements of the plan that were very good and would improve instruction. They also identified requirements that they knew could not work and would actually create more problems for students. They weren't resisting change. They were experienced teachers who understood their classroom dynamics. Their comments were valuable feedback but there was no one to tell. Classroom teachers were not being consulted about these changes and the consequences were alarming.

In the spring of 1998, I conducted a pilot study on the results of the national reform plan and its state interpretations in the classroom. I invited key teachers who were recognized as leaders in our district to participate in a series of discussion groups and written surveys. Teachers responded very enthusiastically to the pilot and it produced four findings. First, the call for education reform and the construction of its objectives were instituted by external forces. Teachers were not part of the conversations that determined reform plans. Second, new regulations were actually limiting the work of these teachers. They were scrambling with increasing time constraints, paperwork, and standardized expectations that were changing what they taught and how they taught it. Third, there were growing frustrations and antagonisms in interpersonal relationships for teachers as they complained of increasing stresses with students who demanded too much, parents who were unreasonable, and authorities who did not support them. Last, I saw teacher morale deflated as they described discouragement, lost meaning in their work, and disconnection with their profession.

I began exploring the phenomenon of the role of classroom teachers in state and national reform. I was curious to know how federal and state reform looked to teachers. Who did they see as having the power to define change? Did controls that limited teacher involvement really exist? When teachers were given a role in these changes, how was it defined? Who defined those limits? What role did teachers play and who decided that? If teachers could participate in reform conversations, what would they say? What do they see as the "problems" in their schools and how do they think those problems should be addressed? These questions were my impetus for further investigation.

LIVE FREE OR DIE

In the summer of 1998, I moved to New Hampshire and resumed my research on the effects of national and state reform for teachers. I came with the intention of finding teachers who were leaders in the state reform effort and recognized as master teachers in their districts. Coming from a state with "Land of 10,000 Lakes" on its license plates, I was curious how teachers from a state with the motto "Live Free or Die" might interpret a nationally defined reform agenda.

Newspapers and local authorities gave me my first insights into the power struggles that were changing political thought about education in New Hampshire. In what I would come to understand as true "Live Free or Die" tradition, the state legislature was in heated debate over adopting a resolution calling for the abolishment of the U.S. Department of Education while also voting to participate in the Goals 2000 program. Governor Stephen Merrill argued against the state legislature agreeing to participate in the federal program:

> Neither the Governor nor the General Court (legislature) is authorized to accept participation in the Goals 2000 program. The State Board of Education, a citizen board composed of volunteers, is the state educational agency authorized under the Goals 2000 legislation to accept or decline funding. I believe the house bill would effectively override the board's authority to discuss, debate, and eventually vote on whether our state should become involved with this federal program. (Sommerfield, 1996, p. 22)

A representative from the New Hampshire Department of Education responded to the governor's argument:

> We couldn't believe he said that! We need the money and stopping the bill took funds away from districts that really needed the support. This was sort of a "last straw" for people who supported education in the state. (06-1-7)

A high school principal felt the same way:

> You know, we're not a state where, you know, when you have a chance to work on something, we should be free to be active to do that. We have a budget, but if we can get another $10,000.00, why wouldn't we want to? Every educator I know was upset over the stand of the Governor and the board of educators. (03-1-12)

As I witnessed these debates, I wondered if other conversations had occurred that critically examined the actual merits of the Goals 2000 plan and its impact on state education policy. For the purposes of this study, I wondered how it happened that state legislators became the authorities who would decide on a plan designed to "fix" the problems in the state's schools. Where were the teachers and other education specialists in these conversations? Perhaps most importantly, who was considering what was really happening in this contest between state ideology, teachers' professional perspective, and the allure of federal dollars?

SPEAKING FOR TEACHERS

Many people in this study spoke with authority for teachers. Powerful people on the state and local levels described what teachers thought, what teachers needed, and why the work of teachers required "reforming." Administrators and state-level policy makers assured me that the reform plan was necessary and that "good" teachers agreed with and supported the changes.

Highly interesting but also frustrating was the difficulty I had attaining access to teachers to discuss their thoughts. Early attempts to talk to teachers in their buildings were derailed by administrators who were very resistant to my efforts. They based their reluctance on their concerns for teacher "overload," the added stress of being part of a study, or scheduling problems too complex to add one more thing to the school day:

> Yes, I'd like to agree with you coming into our school to talk with teachers but right now we are involved in so many projects, the teachers are just too busy. A couple of teachers might, but we are involved in contract negotiations and I just can't ask them to do another thing. (03-1-2)

> I would love to tell you that it would be fine for you to meet with our teachers, but I can't. They are too busy to meet with you and I couldn't burden them. (1-2-9)

> Well, if you ask them to do it, it stops being voluntary. They will feel like they should. I don't want to add to that burden on them. Our teachers are doing fine . . . they feel fine that they have input already. (03-1-5)

> Our teachers are very busy. They don't have the time to attend discussion groups or be interviewed on top of everything else they have to do. (02-1-9)

> Well, I'm very sorry to tell you that it will not work here. I know my teachers are overloaded [laughs]. I know it probably sounds funny that teachers here don't have the time to talk about pressures and reform agendas, but it's true. They are too overloaded to talk about what is going on [laughs, again]. (01-1-13)

This is contrasted to what teachers said when I approached them outside of school about participating in this study:

> Oh, you will get a strong response. Teachers are so strained by what is going on. Parents are driving us crazy and there is no time to get everything done. You know how it is. . . . They just keep piling more and more on us—we don't even have time to think anymore. (01-2-9)

> Absolutely! Nobody ever asks us what we think about anything. They just tell us what we are supposed to do. . . . We aren't ever involved in decisions about change because we are just too busy. There's no time to talk. (01-2-3)

> We don't want to talk? That's a crock! He (the administrator) probably didn't even listen to you. He never listens to anybody. My feeling is that he doesn't want you to have access to what we would say. And it's that simple. If he was going to let you talk to us, he would want to "front load" us first and he didn't want to have to do that. (01-2-6)

> I would participate and so would a lot of other people. We are all so frustrated with what is going on and we have nothing to say about any of it. Let me know when you want to start. I'll start talking with other teachers. (02-13-7)

The control over teachers was further evidenced when I finally did get a principal to agree to let me distribute surveys:

> I called our superintendent because he should know what is going on. Our teachers are very stressed and overworked. He thinks if you want to send a letter to the teachers, it is okay with him so it is okay with me. I can't guarantee much of a response from them. They are very busy with everything they have to do. I want a copy of the survey and the letter. Nothing gets distributed to them without my okay. (02-1-8)

I convinced a second principal to let me conduct a panel discussion in her building to discuss how teachers were implementing reform. The principal chose the participants:

I will set up a panel for you. I have a curriculum facilitator, an assistant principal, reading director, and a few others who could answer your questions.
I will be there, too. (03-2-15)

These early efforts and discussions were a foreshadowing of the tensions
that were to emerge between teachers and their authorities.

Over the course of the next year, I interviewed classroom teachers,
school administrators, union officials, parents, and State Department of
Education representatives. I conducted panel interviews and individual interviews. I traveled around the state and visited wealthy districts and districts struggling for adequate funding. Consistently, teachers described a
taxonomy of power in their schools and districts that excluded them from
meaningful dialogue about mandated reform changes. They had no problem identifying the issues and the real needs of their classrooms. School
administrators spoke frankly about the reality of being torn between district pressures and state politics as they tried to manage their buildings.
And, I met with state education officials who felt consumed by a new culture of politicking that prohibited them from meaningful reflection and re-
sponsive leadership. The story of education reform that had started in
Minnesota continued.

DON'T MESS WITH TEXAS

In 2002, I moved to Texas. For a Yankee girl, this change of scene was in-
triguing and offered an interesting opportunity to add the perspective of
teachers from a state unique in its politics and well-known for its national
leadership. NCLB was signed into law that year and education reform had
taken on a whole new focus of increased controls on learning and high-
stakes testing. Most significantly, the pressure on teachers had increased.
Accountability now included stark tones of severe consequences that tied
student test scores directly into individual teacher evaluations and, ultimately, the future of their own schools.

Undaunted by the "Don't Mess with Texas" state bumper stickers, I
jumped into the interview process as a practiced veteran! It didn't take long
to identify top-scoring school districts, inner-city districts, and districts

from rural communities. Within those communities, I located "master teachers" through referrals from parents, superintendents, and other teachers. I looked for teachers who were recognized in local publications and teachers who were voted "teacher of the year" in their districts. I announced the intentions and history of this study at education seminars and invited interested people to participate. The number of responses and people who wanted to be interviewed was almost overwhelming. The study was extended by another year.

The observations and stories from Texas were powerful and timely additions to the ones I had already collected in Minnesota and New Hampshire. Minnesota teachers were new to reform changes and had accurately predicted many of the results teachers in New Hampshire were experiencing. Texas teachers provided confirmation of many of the New Hampshire teachers' conclusions but added their valuable perspectives on NCLB. The punitive undercurrents of NCLB were a consistent topic for these teachers and were described on all levels. Texas teachers also added the disturbing dimension of the impact of high-stakes testing on children. Together, these teachers from three very different states told remarkably similar stories that confirmed my original thoughts. Teachers weren't being heard and they had a lot to say!

TEACHERS' VOICES

Classroom teachers in Minnesota, New Hampshire, and Texas told me their stories. Their narratives are candid, often impassioned, and many times troubling. They describe what is really happening to them as they work to accommodate federal reform policy. These teachers describe reform efforts that may be well-intentioned but that have resulted in serious and far-reaching consequences. They feel they have been robbed of their professional authority in their classrooms and they feel many of the changes they are required to assimilate are undermining their work.

Three principal points emerge from this study and will be examined in the following chapters. First, the current reform plan, by its construction and intentions, does not provide a role for teachers as definers or contributors in its evolution. Second, the federal reform plan contains erroneous and misleading assumptions that promise results that cannot be uniformly achieved. Third, the reform plan and its enforcements have deskilled teachers and compromised learning for students.

ORGANIZATION OF THE BOOK

This study explores what classroom teachers are experiencing as they attempt to meet federal and state reform requirements. The book is divided into four themes. Part I is an overview of the history and evolution of the national reform movement spanning the past 25 years. Chapter 2 details the causes and resulting forces of change that set into motion the reform policies classroom teachers across the country are now implementing.

Part II presents the impact of reform policies on teaching and learning. Chapter 3 looks at the dramatic shift in how curriculum is viewed, written, and delivered. Teachers evaluate curriculum standards, the changes in teaching priorities, and revised instructional strategies that follow test-driven curriculum. Teachers' perceptions of a "crisis of time" are studied and teachers describe how a school day actually runs.

High-stakes testing and its consequences in the classroom and in the community are the focus of chapter 4. The purposes of state testing are discussed. Teachers evaluate the test's validity and its reliability as an indicator of authentic learning. Time is considered, again, as teachers discuss the loss of teaching time now dedicated to lengthy test preparations.

Part III focuses on changes in teachers' perceptions of their profession and their responsibilities. Chapter 5 begins with a sobering look at what is happening as reform pressures impact the ways teachers and students relate in the classroom. The serious effects of aligning teacher quality with student test scores are examined. Teachers speak frankly about special education requirements and the impact in the classroom of students with high needs.

An important goal of NCLB is the promise of a "highly qualified" teacher in every classroom. Chapter 6 examines what this means to teachers as they evaluate what they see as strengths in their profession as well as weaknesses. They provide recommendations on how entrance requirements can be improved as well as ways their own professional development could be better supported.

Chapter 7 returns to the question of why teachers are not participating in the decisions behind the reform process. Teachers share their personal experiences on the local and state levels as to how reform policy was designed and is now implemented. Administrators and state officials join in the conversation describing the methods used to introduce reform plans and ways those intentions continue to be monitored.

The final section looks at the future of reform. Chapter 8 begins with a review of the current reform structure. It identifies elements in the reform package that have resulted in positive changes for schools as well as changes that teachers believe have hurt public education. Fundamental assumptions in the current reform package are examined as well as promises that cannot be kept. Teachers speak candidly to policy makers about the changes they feel must occur. The chapter concludes with recommendations for authentic policy revisions that include a new role for teachers in the definitions of education reform.

It is my hope and intention that this book adequately and fairly represents all sides of this complicated but important national reform effort to improve the educational opportunities for all children. I am convinced that this significant goal can only be achieved when all participants have a voice in identifying what the real problems are, what is missing in the education equation, and what steps need to be taken to move schools forward. This book is not written to provide all of the answers to the problems currently plaguing reform efforts. It is written to add a very important perspective to the conversation. With this goal in mind, I present the voices of classroom teachers from Minnesota, New Hampshire, and Texas with sincere gratitude for their valuable time, their dedication to their profession, and their willingness to share their experiences.

2

A Brief History of Education Reform

What we expect from our schools and what we consider a good education reflect the political climate of the times. Education policy and decision-making systems have always aligned with the needs of the community that provided the financing. Throughout most of our history, the federal government has left school decisions to the states and the local school districts. Not surprisingly, education standards and opportunity have varied considerably from state to state depending on the wealth and resources available.

It wasn't until the early 1970s that the federal government got involved in the schools through the offer of additional revenues attached to special education requirements. Most states readily accepted the support. The 1980s brought the most severe economic recession the country had experienced since the Great Depression. The resulting financial struggles faced by communities and their schools set the stage for a new power relationship linking federal authority to define guidelines with the willingness of states and school districts to comply.

It was during this time of upheaval that the political and business communities turned their focus on the relationship education played in ensuring a competitive edge on a global scale. A flurry of studies and reports were produced at this time but none rocked the foundations of schools like *A Nation at Risk*, written by the National Commission on Excellence in Education and released to the public in 1983. With inflammatory and militaristic language,

If gov't had not become involved in education in the 70s, where would we be today?

was gov't involvement inevitable?

A Nation at Risk set off a national alarm that received swift reactions from a struggling populace.

> Our nation is at risk. What was unimaginable a generation ago has begun to occur—others are matching and surpassing our educational attainments. If an unfriendly foreign power had attempted to impose on America the mediocre educational performance that exists today, we might well have viewed it as an act of war. (National Commission on Excellence in Education, 1983, p. 5)

The commission determined that public schools were failing to educate students to a level that could support a global job market. Comparative test scores indicated American students trailing students of other industrialized nations. Commissioners questioned whether we were capable of meeting the exploding technological advancements of East Asia. It was concluded that current practices of instruction, depth of curriculum, and systems of assessment were not producing a labor pool that could ensure a return to economic competition and fiscal security. The business community and the government joined forces in a common effort to reform education and policy. As the reports rolled in and committees evaluated next steps, teachers became the main focus of scrutiny and accountability.

REFORM OF THE 1980S

The first wave of reform occurred between 1982 and 1983. Following the prescriptions of *A Nation at Risk*, reform efforts centralized control on the state level. They focused on the pursuit of "excellence" through state mandates intensifying much of what was already in place (National Commission on Excellence in Education, 1983). Recommendations included higher graduation requirements, more testing, and a more standardized curriculum.

In contrast, the next wave (1983–1989) looked at ways to professionalize teaching and restructure schools. These reformers called for a total restructuring of the educational system:

> Much of the rhetoric of the recent education reform movement has been couched in the language of decline, suggesting that standards have slipped, that the education system has grown lax and needed to return to some ear-

lier performance standard to succeed. Our view is very different. We do not believe the educational system needs repairing; we believe it must be rebuilt to match the drastic change needed in our economy if we are to prepare our children for productive lives in the 21st century. (Carnegie Forum on Education and the Economy, 1986, p. 14)

Responding to the Carnegie Forum report, *A Nation Prepared* (1986), and the National Governors' Association report, *Time for Results* (1986), the second wave concluded that decentralization of power, flexibility in problem solving, and autonomy for teachers and school districts were essential to meet the divergent learning needs of the current student populations.

The role of classroom teachers was also scrutinized in the second wave. A new "professionalization" that included higher standards in teacher preparation was called for. Teacher accreditation was redefined as including strategies to monitor individual teacher performance with accountability measures to ensure results. A major policy mechanism also involved a new distribution of power in which parents and teachers worked together on school decisions through site-based governance models offering parents new opportunities to become directly involved in school decisions.

School districts and local constituents were receptive to new ways of looking at funding and decision making in the 1980s. Many districts were struggling with diminished revenues as local real estate taxes were impacted by the effects of depressed housing markets. Households were resistant to increasing real estate taxes to stabilize local tax revenues or fund district change initiatives that would support the call for school reform. Growing school populations and expanding special education costs added to the increasingly strained and already limited school budgets. This escalating crisis of expanded fiscal needs and dwindling resources set the stage for a shift in ideology and public sentiment that cemented federal authority over local schools.

National policy makers came forward with powerful recommendations for redefinition of public education. New ways of defining expectations for classroom teachers were fundamental in these plans. In the first wave, a new state-level authority was recommended, using mandates to define curriculum choice and testing standards. The second wave followed with recommendations of greater teacher authority over curriculum and instruction decisions, improved training of teachers, and a restructuring of schools to provide greater flexibility. This contradiction of greater control over teachers on the state level while granting teachers more autonomy in the classroom created a conflict of roles for teachers that was described by one researcher as the "San Andreas fault in education reform," with classroom teachers trapped in its center (Murphy, 1990).

THE EVOLUTION OF FEDERAL POLICY

President George Bush initiated federal action in education policy in 1989 at the national education summit in Charlottesville, Virginia. Governors from all 50 states participated in the summit (U.S. Department of Education, 1991a). They drafted a four-part framework for a federal education reform plan. First, they determined that national intervention was required to align local standards with the world standards of our economic competitors. Second, they identified a need for a system of standardized criteria-referenced testing. Third, they contended that school districts were misleading parents about the true achievement of their children. Specific national standards were needed for parents to measure their children's achievement against other children around the country. Last, they concluded existing test practices did not hold high enough stakes for students. Employers needed assessments they could interpret to accurately indicate job readiness (U.S. Department of Education, 1991a). The governors' findings were formalized in a document prepared by the secretary of education and submitted to President Bush. The document established "new world standards" for American students:

> Standards will be developed for each of the five core subjects that represent what young Americans need to know and be able to do if they are to live and work successfully in today's world. These standards will incorporate both knowledge and skills to ensure that, when they leave school, young Americans are prepared for future study and the work force. (U.S. Department of Education, 1991a, p. 11)

GOALS 2000: EDUCATE AMERICA ACT

Bill Clinton was one of the governors who participated in drafting the Charlottesville statement. In 1993, the newly elected President Clinton presented

[Handwritten margin note: What about students who do not perform well on tests? This does not mean they are or will be incompetent in the world force.]

the Goals 2000: Educate America Act to the country. Included in the act was a requested $420 million for the first year of the program to be awarded in the form of grants to states who voluntarily agreed to adopt their own standards and assessments consistent with national recommendations.

States were asked to design their own education improvement plans that reflected national recommendations. For the first time in our history, state legislators throughout the country became directly involved in decisions that would shape new interpretations of the ways schools could define success and how teachers would be directed in their work.

The Goals 2000: Educate America Act also revolutionized how education policy would be designed. Local school districts now came under the authority of a centralized, top-down governance model. In this hierarchy, the federal government established academic standards and objectives for the states. The states followed with legislated standards for the individual school districts. School district authorities outlined them for principals and principals interpreted them for teachers.

Relinquishing local control of curriculum decisions, states were encouraged to develop improvement plans that would set the national curriculum standards as goals for all districts. Community participation was encouraged as states and later districts met to plan how they would incorporate these new standards into district curriculum. Federal guidelines were provided to encourage the involvement of parents, teachers, and community members in these school reform efforts.

States were also directed to measure the success of their improvement plans by developing a system of state assessments and accountability measures. Historically, districts chose their own assessments and used them to monitor individual student progress and to make informed decisions about curriculum and instructional strategies. The Goals 2000 plan required all students to be tested on the same curriculum goals for the first time in the history of American education. Because all districts were tested on the same goals at the same time, state government agencies and the general public could track the success of each district and each school within each district using the same standard. Additionally, the academic progress of public school students could be federally tracked, measured, and compared in a consistent manner. Not surprisingly, as results of these early testing requirements came in, citizens reasonably questioned why some schools scored so much better than others and why some districts consistently ranked higher than others.

Supports for these efforts were considerable. In addition to the Bush and then Clinton administration, the National School Board Association, the Council of Chief State Offices, and National Governors' Association supported the recommendations made in 1992 for national standards and examinations. Additionally, both teachers' unions, the National Education Association and the American Federation of Teachers, joined in its support (National Council on Education Standards and Testing, 1993).

With the shift in decision-making power, local school boards, district authorities, and classroom teachers relinquished the authority to set their own curriculum standards. They also lost authority over the pacing of instruction and assessment for their communities. National curriculum committees identified the knowledge all students should know before they graduated from high school. The National Science Board (1983) summarized the rationale behind this change in a tone of urgency:

> The nation is failing to provide its children with the intellectual tools needed for the 21st century. By 1995, the nation must provide for all its youth, a level of mathematics, science, and technology education that is the finest in the world.

For classroom teachers, Goals 2000 provided clear guidelines for curriculum consistency and established, regulated testing procedures.

The establishment of national goals set a standard that received endorsements from government education agencies, business leaders, and the teachers' unions. But not all educators were convinced that a uniform approach to education would solve the problems in America's schools. Questions began to surface about whether or not all students should have the same curriculum and if a set assessment schedule was in the best interests of everyone. Published test scores comparing individual schools and measuring districts against districts fueled heated debate over issues of unequal funding and resources, discrepancies in spending, and the growing complexity of special-needs and at-risk students. With diminished authority over their work, teachers were caught in a growing debate over meaningful change in their work and attainable results.

COMPREHENSIVE SCHOOL REFORM

In answer to the complaint that reform packages tend to be single-focused, Congress launched the Comprehensive School Reform Demonstration (CSRD) program in 1998. The CSRD was based on a systemwide vision of reform that blended school issues with government policy. Basically, the plan allowed schools eligible for Title I funds and other public schools to access funds for costs related to specific products and services. Start-up costs for districts were considerable, ranging between $45,000 and $588,000. Schools were required to fund teacher training and planning, professional development, technology upgrades, and travel. In 2002, this program became a permanent part of the Elementary and Secondary Education Act with funding increased from $265 million to $310 million. For many districts that were already struggling to balance budgets, the financial gains of CSRD did not equal the costs to qualify.

NO CHILD LEFT BEHIND ACT OF 2002

On January 8, 2002, President George W. Bush expanded on the intentions of Goals 2000 when he signed the No Child Left Behind Act (NCLB) into law. It focuses on four basic principles: accountability for results, expanded options for parents of students in failing schools, an emphasis on teacher training and teaching methods backed by current research as best practices, and expanded flexibility and local control over the spending of some federal dollars.

> This plan is a promise to our children and their parents and to our young people seeking higher education. We promise to improve the quality of education and to raise our expectations of what students can accomplish. We promise to leave no student behind. And in return, this nation may ask our young people to use their skills and knowledge to defend our citizens, to contribute to our economy, to rebuild our communities and to strengthen our democracy. (U.S. Department of Education, 2002, p. iv)

NCLB is a dramatic next step in the role of standards and the interpretation of accountability in public school education. While accountability

criteria have been debated in each reform initiative, NCLB shifts the focus of accountability from "proof of effort" on the part of districts to
"demonstration of success" through student achievement as determined
through state testing programs. NCLB requires states to provide proof that
all students are reading on grade level by the third grade, attaining strong
academic knowledge and skills within 12 years of public education, and
graduating from high school (U.S. Department of Education, 2002).

. The federal government has ensured state compliance with the regulations of NCLB by tying it to the powerful Elementary and Secondary Education Act (ESEA). This act supports and regulates the majority of federal K–12 programs in public schools. The law is divided into sections, or
titles. Title I of the ESEA originated in 1965. Its purpose is to provide
funds to support and improve achievement of poor and disadvantaged students. It is important to note that the general population of students is not
eligible for these funds. The reauthorization of the law in 2001 increased
its allocations to nearly $13 billion in grants for fiscal year 2002. By 2006,
the education budget expanded to include $12.7 billion for Title I grants
to districts, $11.4 million for Individuals with Disabilities Education Act
(IDEA) grants to states, $32 million for advanced placement classes, and
$11.3 billion for vocational education.

When the ESEA was reauthorized in 2001, the federal government's
authority over schools expanded to include all students attending a
school receiving Title I funds. This shift radically changed accountability in public education. Under the new rules, all students in a Title I
building, regardless of whether they were identified for Title I services or
not, were now required to take state assessments and all students had to
show evidence of adequate yearly progress. It was further required that
test results would be disaggregated and reported based on students' race,
poverty level, English language ability, and disabilities. These subgroups
were to be held to the same standards as the rest of the population and
would contribute to the ultimate determination of a school's success or
failure.

NCLB also includes a commitment to community awareness and parent empowerment. Districts are required to make test scores easily acces-
sible to the public. Additionally, annual report cards on each school's performance began publication in the 2002–2003 school year. These report
cards provide school and district comparisons of student achievement on

state tests as well as comparisons on graduation rates, schools that are identified as "in need of improvement," and the professional qualifications of teachers. State report cards also provide a venue to track and compare the progress of each state using the same criteria. Based on yearly test results, we now have the capability of comparing students in Alabama to students in Alaska and anywhere in between.

To qualify for federal funding, states are required to hold schools accountable for all students reaching the state-defined "proficient" level within 12 years. For those schools not meeting NCLB, there are built-in consequences and sanctions. After two years of not demonstrating improvement, failing schools are required to provide supplemental services to failing students including tutoring, after-school services, and summer school programs. Funding for these supports comes from a percentage of the school's Title I funds. Each successive year of school failure results in more stringent sanctions. The NCLB plan also provides options for parents of students in failing schools. Parents are allowed to transfer their child to a more successful public or charter school with vouchers. A percentage of the home school's Title I funds is to be used to cover transportation for these students. Federal support for charter schools is also expanded to provide greater opportunities to create new charter schools.

The NCLB act requires a "highly qualified teacher in every classroom." Public elementary or secondary school teachers must be licensed and certified by the state (U.S. Department of Education, 2002, p. 2). The plan recommends improved teacher training with greater access to current education research and best practices along with more rigorous state teacher certification exams. New elementary teachers must demonstrate subject matter and teaching skills in the areas of basic elementary school curriculum. Secondary teachers must demonstrate a high level of competency in each academic subject taught. Research-based reading instruction is also added to state teacher certification requirements.

Practicing teachers are also included in new regulations. The law requires each state to develop and submit to the U.S. secretary of education a plan to ensure that all teachers in the state who are teaching core academic subjects (e.g., English, math, science, social studies, foreign languages, art) meet the "highly qualified" criteria by the 2005–2006 school year. School districts are encouraged to link research-based instructional practices to professional development opportunities. Alternative compensation plans are also recommended for consideration:

> By working with the states and by highlighting promising practices, we will encourage the development of alternative compensation systems (such as those based on student achievement and those allowing differential pay for high-need areas), as well as accountability systems linked to student achievement gains. The Department will examine tenure systems and will promote alternatives. Information about teacher qualifications will be made public to parents through school report cards, as required by "No Child Left Behind." (U.S. Department of Education, 2002, p. 41)

NCLB also provides increased flexibility in the ways states and districts can spend federal dollars. States and school districts have the authority to shift up to 50% of allocated funds to other specific federal education programs. Options include teacher training, technology, Safe and Drug Free Schools, 21st Century Community Learning Centers, and the Innovative Programs block grants. Local districts are also granted some flexibility on how they will allocate some funds without being required to get state approval. Local discretion becomes limited if a school is identified in the "school improvement" stage.

PUBLIC RESPONSE TO REFORM POLICY

Public awareness and support of the extensive reform efforts launched in 1983 varies by topic. Despite the considerable economic and political swings since the early 1980s, Americans remain committed to education and its improvement. Educational Testing Service found that 52% of the adults surveyed in 2002 confirmed a need for "major changes or a complete overhaul" in our current education system (p. 2). Interestingly, most people did not think there were problems in their own schools. Seventy-one percent of public school parents gave their oldest child's school an "A" or "B" while giving neighboring schools a "C" or lower. This is up from parents' ranking of the same criteria at 66% in 1992. Americans are also committed to paying for reform. Seventy-eight percent said they wanted to see reduced spending in other areas before cutting education spending. State and federal legislators should note that 58% said they were willing to raise taxes rather than cut current education spending (Rose & Gallup, 2002).

Americans also endorse state and national controls on curriculum standards and accountability measures. Seventy-three percent of adults believe teachers and administrators are responsible for student learning (Educational Testing Services, 2002). For schools that do not meet state standards, 56% of adults support termination of the teachers and school officials (Rose & Gallup, 2002). While supporting school sanctions for poor performance, parents also agree that the gap between achievement of white and black and Hispanic students is not related to the quality of the school and its teachers. Rather, they ranked factors related to home life, economic disadvantage, and poor community environment as the top reasons for achievement gaps in high-risk populations. Similarly, 39% of parents and 58% of teachers list parents' lack of involvement as the top problem facing schools today (Education Testing Services, 2002).

Perhaps most startling of all findings is how unaware many people actually are of the status of the national reform plan and its impact in our schools. Education Testing Services in 2002 found that only 12% of adults and 36% of educators knew that NCLB had been passed by Congress and signed by the president. A sizable 47% of all adults and 36% of educators felt that there was "a lot of talk but no action so far" on a national education reform plan (p. 5).

Despite the low level of public awareness of the actual reform document and changes in leadership, the past 20 years have produced an escalating reform effort that has taken on a force of its own in America's classrooms. The shift of decision-making power from local agencies to the federal and state levels has caused a reinterpretation of how education policy is made, who enforces it, and how it is translated into implementation in the classrooms.

Today, curriculum controls are set outside of the classroom and testing schedules are assigned by state government officials. Successful teachers deliver instruction in a timely and efficient manner. Government agencies monitor each school's progress based on state goals. Built-in sanctions and fiscal penalties provide options and supports for students from schools identified as failing. Standardized test scores serve the dual purposes of measuring appropriate yearly progress for each student as well as defining accountability standards for teachers and, ultimately, their schools. In the next chapters, we will look at what teachers have to say about these changes and what they say has happened to their profession.

II

The Impact of Reform Policies on Teaching and Learning

3

Teaching for Improved Student Achievement

The key focus of the No Child Left Behind (NCLB) plan is to ensure that all learners have access to instruction that will provide 12 years of monitored progress and academic achievement. Achievement is defined as learning a set curriculum based on predetermined state standards followed by measurement of that learning through standardized, regularly scheduled assessments. Controls are in place to define, regulate, and monitor the work of classroom teachers on all grade levels. Fiscal incentives, structured government supports, and clearly defined consequences are in place to support district cooperation and teacher compliance. The success of this plan rests on an underlying assumption that these new regulators will focus teacher and student efforts in a direction that assures improved levels of student performance.

In this chapter, we move from considering the intentions of the reform effort to examining its implementation. Classroom teachers are central in this examination. We will examine what these changes mean for teachers as they have shifted from participating in their own curriculum decisions to following uniform, state-defined curriculum standards. We will identify the ways that reform has changed the ways teachers design daily lessons, structure instruction, approach individual learning needs of students, and define success. We will look at what these teachers feel is working for them as they implement reform plans and what they feel is actually interfering with their success and the success of their students.

CURRICULUM STANDARDS

Historically, curriculum decisions have been made by district officials and classroom teachers. Districts have based these decisions on a spectrum of criteria ranging from state and local curriculum guidelines, to specific population needs, to budgetary restrictions. Districts have had the flexibility to choose their own tools to measure the success of their efforts, determine who they would test and when, and control how the information would be used and distributed. NCLB standardized these decisions by requiring states to regulate curriculum standards based on national recommendations and requiring districts to use standardized tests to measure success.

Teachers support curriculum standards and they believe these standards have had a positive impact on their teaching. In a national survey done by *Education Week*, 87% of the teachers agreed that raising standards was very much or somewhat a move in the right direction, and 64% felt that coursework had become more challenging in the past three years as a result of the focus on standards (Gandal & Vranek, 2001).

A teacher from a large school district explained how she saw value in these changes:

> It is definitely a change for the good. When I first started teaching, there was no plan in curriculum. Teachers did what they wanted to do. Now we teach everything in the same sequence. So students who switch schools have a better chance of learning. I am more accountable. I know precisely what these kids need and I have the materials to do that. Before, we not only didn't know what curriculum to teach, we also had to come up with our own materials. I like it better this way. I think students have a clearer picture of what is expected of them. (11-1-18)

Described as "change for the good," the benefits of identified curriculum, consistency in grade level instructional goals, and district support of materials were seen by this teacher as promoting better teaching and learning for students.

Teachers feel that they understand the standards and are doing a good job of implementing them into their curriculum. In a national survey done for *Education Week* in 2000, 60% of teachers said that they had developed units and lessons linked to state standards and were comfortable with their own understanding of their state's goals. They also felt state standards made their curriculum more demanding and increased their expectations of their students.

In the same study by *Education Week* and confirmed in this study, elementary and secondary teachers differed on how they see the effects of standardized curriculum in their work. Elementary teachers indicated a direct relationship between standards and improved student effort and performance in their schools. Despite these improvements, they felt that some state standards are too high.

> I don't think that the developmental stages of students were considered when some of the standards were written. You can teach some concepts using every strategy known to man and some kids aren't going to get it. They just aren't ready. I would think the people thinking up these standards would recognize that and make adjustments for those differences. (04-5-12)

Middle school teachers reported higher expectations due to standards but did not feel that their students were responding by working harder. The emotional and social challenges of early adolescence were considered. The teachers did see improvements in efforts to collaborate with other teachers when planning curriculum. They felt this helped to unify teachers' objectives and goals. They also reported improvements in student reading and writing.

> We are definitely seeing improvements in skill levels from the elementary schools. That is making a big difference in what we can do once they get here. I think that is because we are working together better with the lower grades and the expectations are clearer for everyone. Middle school kids have a lot on their minds besides school. We have to keep things very interesting to compete with everything else going on in their heads. (05-3-12)

High school teachers felt the least affected by reform requirements. These teachers described the fewest adjustments in lesson design and modified teaching strategies. Many high school classes are offered in sequence and established levels of difficulty. This structure lessens the need to adapt strategies for learning differences. High school teachers agreed that their teaching strategies tended to be less varied.

> Teachers use much more of a lecture approach in high school for two reasons. First, you have teachers who are majors in their curriculum like chemistry or biology. They are going to go into much more detail about their subjects. They

tend to teach the way they were taught in college. Second, you have to cover so much more detail in high school than in middle school. It takes a long time to cover everything. Strategies like exploration or inquiry methods don't work. Students can't explore or teach each other because there is so much knowledge they need first. (12-04-12).

These teachers also reported the lowest level of improvements in student effort or learning. The majority of high school teachers, however, felt that their students could meet the standards on the state tests.

In addition to supporting curriculum standards that are more challenging, teachers also spoke of the importance of consistency in expectations found in the new standards.

Having consistency in curriculum is absolutely a good thing. We have kids who move around so much. A change in schools used to set a child back. Too often, whole units were missed because there was no consistency in what was taught from one district to the next. I've worked in districts where we couldn't even count on consistency from one building to the next! Now a child has a better chance of getting at least the basics regardless of what his family is doing or where they are living. I also like that every teacher knows exactly what must be covered before the year is over. It might seem funny, but that wasn't always the case before. (12-05-01)

Standardized curriculum goals have provided uniformity in school expectations and provided the community with a definable structure that leads to the successful completion of a body of knowledge for graduating seniors.

TEST-DRIVEN CURRICULUM: WE JUST CAN'T TEACH LIKE WE USED TO

While national standards steer curriculum decisions, standardized testing drives the initiative and determines accountability. To create a culture of achievement, we must demonstrate that achievement counts, at the local, state, and federal levels. We will work with our partners to make accountability for results the hallmark of our education system (U.S. Department of Education, 2002). NCLB expands the purpose of testing from simply providing feedback to parents on student progress to also being the principal definer of teacher and district competency. The effects of this focus are profound. Teachers in this study agreed that test scores dominated decisions about their work.

> Everything about what and how I teach has been changed since the state tests. The entire curriculum for the entire district has been changed. We don't add curriculum or remove curriculum without referencing the test first. (02-2-11)

> I used to have some great units that kids loved and were a change from the regular set content. I just had to stop all of that. We don't study anything that isn't part of the standards anymore. I wish we still had some of that flexibility but we don't. There are too many topics to cover to be adding anything else. (03-5-24)

Fundamental meaning of what teachers teach, how they teach it, and why are reinterpreted in terms of state reform learning standards and accountability criteria. A panel of teachers described the changes in this way:

> What we teach has changed in terms of content. I would say there has been a shift to a more process type of education. One big change is the way we write units. Now we have state curriculum frameworks and they have really made a big difference in how we write our curricula. We make sure that the new curriculum we write is a direct reflection of the frameworks. We want them to score well so we direct our focus to what we know will be on the test. (03-1-12)

In the teacher's words, a "more process type of education" was described, in which teaching strategies reflect a uniformity and conformity in curriculum choice and design. This image of "processing" students takes on tones of a mechanistic view of teaching in which students become part of an input-output model. The instruction defines the input and the standardized tests become the output. These goals reflect the design and focus of the state student assessments.

Teachers have mixed reactions regarding the effects of test-driven curriculum. One teacher who participated in designing the state assessment supported the focus on curriculum frameworks and the change in teaching methods to meet those objectives:

> I know I am biased but I do see some really valuable content changes because of the test and I really do feel that we [are] trying for the right questions that really and truly reflect what we think kids should be able to do. Kids need practice with skills and applications in order to test well. And kids do that by just teaching to certain questions. So I think it is a good test. It really measures what we wanted to do. So I think by all means teach to the test. (03-3-33)

Another teacher saw standards as "raising the bar" for all students. He also saw differences between districts:

> I don't believe in teaching to the test, which I know is going on in many districts. I see standards and testing as raising the bar for all kids. We have motivated kids and parents and I know that makes a big difference. Honestly, most teachers here do high-level teaching anyway, so kids are going to do fine. Whereas, I know in other schools, it's different and the test is a huge issue. I hate the fact that teachers actually feel like they have to teach to the test. (12-04-1)

On the other side of this debate are the consequences of a system of designing curriculum that controls curricular choice, standardizes objectives, and limits instructional strategies for teachers. Teachers were troubled by these changes. They described the effects of test-driven objectives and the loss of flexibility in instructional methods and curriculum design in their classrooms:

> You definitely have to teach to the test. You have to teach what is on the test. You have the option of fitting in anything else you can but there isn't time for much else. You can fit in things here and there for a few minutes [laughs]. But people are definitely eliminating certain things they once taught. The class project kind of thing doesn't happen like it used to because we are covering what is on the test. I think there are lots of good things on the test and I think it helps with a focus. We just can't teach like we used to. The freedom to just think about the needs of your class is gone. (11-1-24)

Teachers in this study were very concerned about the elimination of valued teaching strategies when they contrasted past methodology to current practice. They saw discrepancies emerge between what they defined as competent teaching and what they now saw themselves doing. A primary teacher described how test objectives changed collaborative writing strategies she once used with primary students:

> In our district, the third graders didn't do well on the state test in writing because the format [on the test] was not what they were used to. Now we are changing how we teach writing. We used to do collaborative work with checking each others' work, then editing, then the teacher edits, then the final product. Now we are teaching them to do it alone because that is the test format. And we start it in the first grade. (10-1-56)

A middle school teacher from a high-scoring district described abandoning integrated curriculum strategies:

> A problem is that we were working toward a more integrated curriculum. We liked doing this because it helped students to see real connections between subjects. Now we are shifting away from that. Now that there is more emphasis on specific curriculum from the frameworks, we don't have time to teach those kinds of units. We can't do that, too. We have shifted our focus to match the frameworks. (01-2-50)

Under state and district curriculum controls, teachers felt forced to limit or eliminate teaching strategies such as classroom projects, collaborative work, and integrated curriculum even in cases where these practices reflected sound teaching practice. Educational theorists have also endorsed these methods as model teaching strategies, evidenced in individual and group academic success (Armstrong, 1994; Kozol, 1996; Osterman & Kottkamp, 1993; Tyack & Cuban, 1995). In a panel discussion for this study, teachers repeated their concerns about their loss of professional discretion in instructional decisions and an actual deskilling of teacher performance.

 A second concern for teachers is the way test-driven curriculum can suppress creativity and spontaneity for themselves as well as their students. Teachers described the neutralizing effects of curriculum regulation in their teaching:

> In relation to the innovative, passionate stuff that you like to do which is not found in the frameworks, certainly that has gone to the wayside. That piece

has left for me. Teachers refer to us as sort of clones of each other because we're teaching the same lesson for all of the kids. I can't say everyone is okay with that because there is that piece of losing yourself a little bit, too. (03-1-41)

Another teacher continued:

You know what I am finding? We don't have the fun we used to have. There is no time for that anymore. We can't do the creative type of things we used to do. That's what we had to put aside. You know I find that these kids are still kids. And I find that I am constantly looking at the clock and saying to myself, "We have to get to this and this and this . . ." and I have to stop those conversations we used to have time for. The methods I used to use to teach concepts that were more interesting and really more motivating for kids. You don't have any time for just enjoying being together. (10-1-58)

Teachers' observations were consistent with findings from a study on standardized curriculum done by Cohn and Kottkamp in 1993. The researchers described teachers as "taught" to do their work through state mandate and district-interpreted instructional strategies. Cohn and Kottkamp explain, "When control becomes excessive, teacher autonomy is reduced and learning is suppressed for both students and teachers" (1993, p. 218). They concluded that mandated fundamental skills curriculum forced teachers in their study to deliver the curriculum in ways that generated "passivity, disinterest, and lack of motivation" for both teachers and their students (p. 219).

Regulated delivery of curriculum often disregards the knowledge and professional expertise teachers bring to the classroom:

I have been a teacher for 15 years and teaching is harder for me now than it ever was before. I feel like a first-year teacher because everything I know based on all of my experience is irrelevant now. It doesn't matter if I know a better way to reach kids or if I know a better unit or better format. I have to follow the frameworks and, most of all, I have to do it fast. (10-1-4)

While all teachers identified flexible methodology, creative instruction, and professional experience as important elements of successful teaching, they also acknowledged decreased opportunity to apply these skills or knowledge to their work. Teachers contrasted former teaching strategies they described as interesting and motivating for students to changed methods that were centered on limited objectives, defined by test questions, and abbreviated by restrictive time pressures.

Teachers also talked about the impact of a preset testing schedule that did not necessarily match the best pacing of the class. A veteran elementary teacher provided an example of how she is dealing with this struggle. In a conversation about developing key concepts with students while pacing lessons according to the test calendar, she described the conflict she was facing between her own expertise and knowledge about her students and the confinement of test requirements:

> Teacher: I can be excited about the curriculum and then, boy, suddenly I am thinking, "I have to change my lesson because the test is on Thursday and I haven't gotten the curriculum that far." Professionally, do I "quick teach" so it looks good? Or do I go back with "Okay, I didn't get that far . . . so probably all of the kids are going to miss that question?" It means compromising what is right for their understanding with what the test says they need to know.
>   Interviewer: So are you willing to say, "No, I'm going to do what I feel is right and ignore the pressure of the test?"
>   Teacher: No, we feel so pressured that the majority of the time, you're going to teach to the test. (09-2-5)

Teachers frequently became very animated as they shared common stories regarding the complexities and frustrations of "teaching to the test." They described futility in trying to teach in ways they often felt were superior while remaining committed to district curriculum outlines and test pressures. They also expressed a sense of resignation that they couldn't change what was happening.

A CRISIS OF TIME

Of all issues raised by teachers, the one that most troubled them and aroused the greatest passions was the frustration of not having enough time to do their jobs. They described formulated timelines to meet assessment schedules, increasingly complex student populations that demanded added planning and teacher focus, added state-mandated curriculum, ongoing interruptions in the school day, and increased responsibilities that took them out of the classroom. Each of these items strained an overburdened teaching day. One teacher confirmed this frustration:

> No, I don't even have close to enough time. Most of the time, I feel like I have 50% of the time I need. I know most teachers would agree with that. That is one of the biggest problems we have. We just don't have enough time and no one is paying attention to this. (11-1-5)

Teachers spoke passionately about their struggles with time limitations that were outside of their control, standardized curriculum goals that did not meet the needs of the students, and the increased challenge of special needs. Teachers know that children learn at different speeds, in different ways, and that these learning capabilities change with each subject. When specific learning goals are targeted for all children, some students will meet that goal quickly while others will require more time. The constant monitoring and adjusting that are required to meet the learning needs of divergent populations are fundamental skills effective teachers share. Preestablished district testing schedules limit teacher discretion to pace lessons based on student progress. Instead, teachers follow a more mechanized approach to lesson pacing, by confining teaching to the time allotted between test dates. Teachers are not allowed the flexibility to teach to students' needs. Teachers report that this contradiction in reform intentions and actual implementation is resulting in some students not having the time they need to learn to mastery:

> Right now, we have a new language arts curriculum that reflects the frameworks. Time is a big problem. We have all of this material we have to get through before the test. It is like a timeline that we can't deviate from. When you go this fast, there is no time to review, reteach, and follow up with kids who aren't getting it because the rest of the class has to keep moving. We can't spend the time we need to get to mastery. We just don't spend the time to do things thoroughly anymore. So, I'm sorry to tell you this, but they just don't learn as well. They may pass the test but they don't really understand it. (11-1-11a, 12b)

These teachers described a shift to "minimal" coverage of material as timelines drove the depth and amount of their instruction.

A literature teacher explained how district timelines have changed her instruction on the secondary level:

> We are in a big time bind. And when you constantly push off from one thing to do the next, you have to change how you teach. I think kids feel that pressure by not being able to take the time to really process what they have learned. If a student is really interested in something, it is very hard to let that child work with that interest. We have to stay focused because we won't cover what needs covering if we let kids explore. For example, every eight weeks we give a literature test. If we don't cover everything on that test ahead of time, there is no way those students will pass. And that is followed by eight more weeks and another test. There is no time to remediate. This is the whole year! There is pressure to at least minimally cover all of it. You have to find ways to make shortcuts. (11-1-21)

Teachers expressed serious concern about abandoning successful teaching strategies in efforts to make teaching time more efficient.

A primary teacher described a recent conversation with teachers in her building about this problem:

> We can't spend time for mastery. We just talked about the writing process at lunch. You need to teach skills, conference with the student, do revisions, brainstorm, work with peers, type on the computer. Well, all of that takes a lot of time and a lot of concentration to learn like that. We know it works but it is a big time investment. I can't do that now. There isn't time for lengthy writing experiences anymore. (11-1-12)

Teachers also worried about the loss of opportunities to expand lessons to include student-generated feedback and exploration. They described how standardized curriculum and increased time limitations restricted opportunities for class discussion and interpretation. An elementary teacher who worked on curriculum planning on the state and district levels discussed this issue. Quoted earlier as supporting test-driven curriculum, she reflected on the impact of time restrictions on her own instruction:

> Part of designing new district curriculum has been the limiting aspects of standards. In our planning, we have taken out those "teachable moments."

They don't exist anymore because you don't have the time [laughter]. You know, you say to the kids, "Yes, I know you are interested in that but you know what? It's not in the book!" Unfortunately, we have tightened up the standards but we have lost something. Actually, we have lost a lot of things. (3-3-80)

A science teacher described how instructional strategies have changed in his department:

There is no time to go off on tangents like you did before. If something comes up that is an offshoot on a topic . . . if it isn't directly related to the framework, you back off now. There just isn't time for those kinds of dialogues with kids. There is just too much at stake. Especially when you know this is the last time they may have access to certain topics. You have to cover it thoroughly and that means no time for other things. And science is changing so rapidly. The amount of information has just escalated. You can't cover it all and yet we are told to figure out a way. (1-2-61)

While teachers described a commitment to following the guidelines of the standards and accepting the structure of the testing schedules, they shared a common concern about the loss of time for remediation and reteaching. All teachers shared worries about those students who need a slower pace. Deviation from the identified curriculum resulted in sacrificed time on standardized curriculum, which ultimately impacted "high-stakes" test scores. Yet, perhaps most frustrating for these teachers was the realization that even when they gave up former pacing, teaching, and testing methods, they still weren't covering everything that was newly required:

Well, what most of us do is we know what is there and what we are supposed to do. We try to do as much of it as we can. And if we can't do it all, we can't do it all. We do what we can do. That's just a fact. And we don't tell the world. You don't advertise that you have ended up skipping something. You don't want that to get out. And you don't do it on purpose. You don't want to have your kids behind or put your kids at risk on the test. And every teacher gets comfortable with that. I don't think there is a single teacher that I know who isn't in that position. None of us has enough time to do what we have to do . . . or can get the kids to a point where we are really comfortable and ready to go on to the next thing. It's always a time crunch. It's always a time push to get things done. (11-1-25a)

Teachers felt time constraints limited their choice of teaching strategies and diminished learning opportunities for their students. They recognized that some of their students were not learning to mastery and they were not able to use their skills to improve the situation. Most disturbing was that they did not feel they had the authority to change what they were seeing:

Well, it would be nice for the kids but you wouldn't be helping yourself any. If they don't get the results they are looking for, they are just going to keep tightening the screw on teachers until you either deliver those numbers or you get out of teaching. There will just be more testing — more of those types of questions to ensure that you are covering what they want. (01-2-63-65)

Controls that force compliance contrary to teacher judgment result in a sense of frustration and impotence for teachers. A high school chemistry teacher continued:

I do not have the time to teach to mastery. I cannot get all of my curriculum done and get it to the depth and complexity that I want to. There is just way too much to cover. I can get them to the point that they walk away with the "big idea" which meets the standards for the state test. I could be giving them so much more but I have come to accept the fact that I cannot teach to the depth and mastery level that I would like to teach. (12-04-08)

In some cases, teachers have made the decision to skip curriculum:

This is a huge problem. It does mean that I don't cover certain things. One of the jokes around here is we have a health program that we are supposed to cover over a long time. A lot of teachers just didn't do it. So the last day of school we are doing a quick synopsis of that program with kids. I have to make choices and that means I am going against what the district tells me that I'm supposed to do. I did not follow the curriculum. I did leave things out of the extra programs that I am supposed to teach and I would do it again. I have a solid reputation and no one questions what I do. Other teachers don't have that autonomy. Most of us do worry about the newer teachers who don't have that. (03-3-84)

Teachers simply do not have the time they need.

In 1991, the Education Council Act authorized the National Education Commission on Time and Learning to examine the use of time and its relationship to learning in public schools. Milton Goldberg, who was also the executive director for *A Nation at Risk* in 1983, was the executive director of the project. This comprehensive study identified the greatest challenges and obstacles facing teachers as they move forward with reform requirements:

> Our conclusions and recommendations speak for themselves. Time is the missing element in our great national debate about learning and the need for higher standards for all students. Our schools and the people involved with them—students, teachers, administrators, parents, and staff—are prisoners of time, captive of the school clock and calendar. We have been asking the impossible of our students—that they learn as much as their foreign peers while spending only half as much time in core academic subjects. The reform movement of the last decade is destined to founder unless it is harnessed to more time for learning. (National Education Commission on Time and Learning, 1994, p. 4)

The commission offered many recommendations, including fewer noninstructional activities in the school day and providing a minimum of 5.5 hours for core academic teaching. Since that time, studies have provided mixed conclusions on what needs to be done to solve the crisis of time for schools and their teachers. One point is certain: Teachers today are called on to do more than ever before with less time and they feel that it is getting worse.

THE STRUCTURE OF THE SCHOOL DAY

American schools in the early 1900s were designed to meet the needs of an agrarian society with a focus on covering basic content or the "three R's" for those students who could attend school regularly. Families were responsible for getting their children to and from school. Children with physical handicaps or learning complications were kept at home or sent to special boarding schools.

Public education in 2007 is a very different experience. All children are eligible for a public education and those with physical handicaps or learning complications are protected by law to be educated in the least restrictive environment. Curriculum has expanded dramatically to include English, history, geography, science, civics, the arts, world languages, physical education, speech, health, technology, consumer science, and mathematics. Schools are also asked to allot time for a variety of topics including safety instruction, drug education, character development, community service, and social wellness. In addition, time is needed for nonacademic activities such as class meetings, student government, pep rallies, school assemblies, student interest groups, lunch, study halls, and homeroom. School districts also report a staggering increase in the number of troubled and at-risk students needing additional time for one-on-one or small group emotional, physical, and instructional supports.

The added curriculum, student interventions, and school functions are significant in supporting our goal of an educated population. We have expanded our purposes and services in public education for good reasons. Unfortunately, we have not expanded the school day to support them. Whatever expectations we pass on to the schools, the school day remains roughly the same as it was a hundred years ago. We are still looking at a 6-hour instructional day and a school year that does not go beyond 180 school days. Additionally, studies indicate that, on average, teachers spend 23% of their classroom time on required, noninstructional activities (Smith, 2000). Teachers questioned these added responsibilities:

> Time is a problem. Teachers always talk about time. You want to teach core curriculum and all of a sudden you have these social issues creeping into the classroom and now there is a bill that says you have to teach, for example, sex education or AIDS. So now you say, "I am teaching things that the family should be responsible for." There is a lot of frustration with that. I wonder what the parent is doing? Something is happening in society where that is breaking up and we are supposed to solve it. (03-3-80)

> We are seeing increasing concerns about covering so many topics we didn't even consider when I first started teaching. For example, now my fifth graders are in the drug unit. We spend six weeks on this subject. I think it's important because kids need this information but it's time taken from everything else I have to do. We don't have the time to lose. So it all comes down to more pressure to teach more things with less time. (01-2-15)

As teachers described the time needed to design instruction to meet state requirements, address student diversity, and proportion time for added mandated curriculum requirements, they also talked about the actual decrease in time they had to answer and plan for these changes in their classrooms:

> We used to have some flexibility to meet with our departments and concentrate on what we felt we needed to get done. That time has been cut way back since standards. Now we spend a lot of our professional days talking about latest state or district requirements, special education changes, or listening to speakers. Most of our team meetings are devoted to specific students or meeting with parents so there really isn't much time left for planning. (05-32-41,43)

Teachers described a sense of being "overloaded" with initiatives that required significant planning time to achieve:

> This year we have eleven initiatives in our building. They are all great ideas and the school board loves them and they sound great on paper and we aren't meeting any of them well. There is way too much politics and politics burns out teachers. They come in with these ideas and we just get to the point where we are starting to make some progress and then they drop the whole idea and start something new. We need to bring something to fruition but that takes time. (05-02-16)

Many teachers also described the loss of planning periods as a part of the growing crisis of available substitute teachers:

> My planning periods depend upon specialists being here to take my students. If the specialists aren't here, we don't get our planning periods. This is a problem in this district because the city cannot get substitute teachers. I have taught other teachers' classes when I have had a student teacher because they couldn't get a sub. They pay us if we lose prep time, which is nice, but I still lose that time. (11-1-9)

> We have a small school and we get a lot of additional duties to cover if someone is sick or out. I may have a period reserved for planning and then I get a call asking me to cover study hall or the lunch room. I don't mind doing it but it means my planning time is gone. (04-03-17)

A notable difference between American schools and schools of other world nations is the fact that American school teachers are interrupted and distracted by ongoing, noncurricular events throughout the course of a day (Berliner & Biddle, 1995). During one group discussion, teachers acknowledged that there was little concern from administration or parents about the impact that distractions and interruptions have on their work:

> I would say at least a half to three-quarters of my lessons are interrupted by messages or office calls or students being pulled out of class for other classes. We have band students leaving for their lessons, special needs kids meeting with their specialists, kids needing medical treatment, early releases, and late comers coming and going all day long not to mention students summoned to the office or other areas of the building for any number of reasons or messengers dropping off or picking up paper work. I can be in the middle of a lesson and the phone will ring or a voice comes over the PA asking for something or someone. Every one of those interruptions stops a lesson and breaks the concentration of the class. (12-14-3)

Daily teaching schedules change to support noncurricular events:

> I have a week's lessons planned out because you have to plan ahead and all of a sudden we get an announcement saying there is no first period today, or we are bumping back third period to make time for a pep rally for basketball or we are shortening all classes for some other event at the end of the day. This kind of stuff happens at least once a week and it throws off a whole week's curriculum. Kids get shortened versions of their classes. It's not right. (12-3-5-7)

Teaching time is also used to handle clerical duties, fundraising efforts, and volunteer services:

> I think too much of the school day is taken up with paperwork or collecting things like lunch money or magazine drive money or sorting book orders or PTO notices. Sometimes, it is like teaching comes last on the list of things we need to get done each day. I have piles of stuff like this all of the time. And I wonder if the taxpayers really want me spending time on this stuff rather than planning for and teaching kids. (11-17-02)

As schools have become more conscious of the need for safety and supervision, teachers have more responsibilities outside of the classroom, usurping time that was once reserved for planning:

> A growing problem is all of the duties we have. When I am not teaching, I have duties. In this school, there are a lot of high-risk kids with serious problems so we have to have a pretty heavy "duty" schedule because we have to maintain a low teacher-student ratio to maintain order. We really work on the school being calm and safe but it means it takes a lot of teachers to make it stay that way. (02-3-8)

> My biggest concern is too many demands on teachers to perform tasks that take away from our primary function, which is to teach. We are spending time, instead, filling out more and more paperwork, fund raising, committee work, calling parents, café duty, playground and bus duty . . . special education meetings every spare minute. We schedule right over lunch. It just doesn't stop. (02-3-8)

Teachers are also called upon to support many of the schoolwide discipline programs. An example is suspension and detention duty:

> We also have in-school suspension that we have to share. This is for things that happen outside of our own classrooms. We have to share that. And then you have the students who have just detention. If they are your students you can do that in your room. That is better because they don't get recess but at least you can work in your room while they serve detention time. (11-1-19)

Office interruptions, student traffic in and out of the room, school assemblies, and added clerical functions all depreciate instructional time. Supervisory duties and staffing shortages impact precious time that should be used for curriculum development and collaborative planning. The realities of the structure of the school day and the mismanagement of teachers' time are very serious issues as we look at reform in the classroom.

TEACHERS WORKING FOR
IMPROVED STUDENT ACHIEVEMENT

Federal mandates tied into much needed fiscal incentives have redefined how teachers approach their work and how their success is measured.

Teachers describe a new "process kind of education" in which students are "moved through" curriculum with regularly scheduled "quality assurance" tests to measure progress and completion of goals. This mechanized approach to teaching has serious flaws for teachers.

Teaching strategies and content have changed. The "student-centered" approaches that support interactive discussions, analysis of ideas, and deductive reasoning are increasingly exchanged for "teacher-centered" instruction in which lessons are designed to focus on very specific objectives in the most efficient and timely manner. Additionally, teachers describe teaching less content by skipping material they once taught if it is not "on the test." They describe teaching material that is fact based, in ways that are less interesting for students, and personally less satisfying for themselves.

The effects of these changes on student mastery of material are considerable. Teachers explain how assessment schedules define when instruction is done and testing begins. They see students' understanding of content compromised as they shift from teaching for mastery to teaching to the common or "passing" level required on the state tests. Equally troubling is the reality of differences in students' capabilities. Preestablished pacing can be too slow for high-ability students and too fast for others.

Time constraints seemed to be teachers' greatest limitation and the source of greatest anxiety. While there is no place in the reform plan in which teachers are told not to practice creativity in their classrooms, or not to make their lessons interesting or not to teach to mastery, teachers describe time constraints as so extreme that there is no time left to teach in ways that are more interesting and successful for their students. Teachers do not have time to plan for the changes reform requires. They don't have time to design instructional strategies that might enhance curricular goals. They don't have time to reach all students and teach to their differences. Restricted and controlled by a continuum timeline of instruction and assessment, teachers and their students have to "keep pushing forward" even when common sense tells them their efforts are being defeated.

On a personal level, teachers also share a sense of "losing some of themselves" in efforts to achieve uniformity in their action. One teacher said they are becoming "sort of clones" of each other as every teacher adopts standardized curriculum, identical objectives, and district assessment schedules in uniform compliance. Additionally, teachers feel their own knowledge and experience has no intrinsic value in state-defined meanings of teacher competency. In a system of regulation, all teachers are measured by the same standards with no opportunity or support for original or creative interpretations of instruction or curriculum.

Standardized curriculum identifies what will be known. It also identifies what would not be known. In this respect, Arons (1994) regarded the establishment of a national curriculum—or of 50 states' curricula—as taking on dangerous tones of control over knowledge and questionable constitutionality. He argues:

> In a pluralistic society, standardized curriculum and value-neutral schooling are as it were contradictions in terms. The fact there has been virtually no public debate about the fate of intellectual freedom and cultural diversity under Goals 2000 does not inspire confidence in the wisdom of this reform program. Nor should those who appreciate the complex connection between democracy and education be reassured by the tacit approval a national curriculum has received from educators. If there are significant reasons for putting the principles of constitutional democracy at risk by creating a national curriculum, they ought to become part of the public discourse before this juggernaut gets under way. (pp. 57–58)

Researchers have also found classroom teachers concerned about the limitations of set standards in the curricular areas. In a study done by Cohn and Kottkamp (1993), teachers did not see curriculum standards as either desirable or necessary. In some subject areas such as science and technology, teachers felt that intellectual developments were moving too rapidly to warrant constraining definitional moves. In a study done by Atkin (1994), teachers worried that something "quite inert, and not animating" would result if government reformers continued to insist on a "single set of standards" to govern their work (p. 67).

Cohn and Kottkamp described teachers as frustrated by narrowly focused curricular objectives. They did not feel connected to their content or engaged in the instructional processes. They felt lessons lacked meaning for themselves and their students. Cohn and Kottkemp concluded that these tensions were having serious effects on teacher morale:

> In the current reform context, it is a case of teachers being told simultaneously that they are responsible for student success or failure because they

have the knowledge, skill, and authority to make the difference, but at the same time, that they must follow the prescriptions of others outside the classroom because they are basically incapable of making fundamental curricular and instructional decisions. These mixed messages are taking a terrible toll on teachers. (p. 250)

Arons (1994) argues that "the more we submit these matters of intellect and conscience to political determination, the less respect for intellectual freedom, cultural diversity, and critical thinking we should expect our children to learn" (p. 56). Other theorists felt that dangerous assumptions were made about what was the right curriculum and which curriculum could be forfeited for school districts that represented diverse populations with very different learning and social needs (Apple, 1990; Loveless, 1994).

Teachers in this study see value in identifying common curricula with similar goals on each grade level. They support using assessments that support the goals. Teachers argue against controls that limit their skills and disregard the professional expertise they bring to their classrooms. They describe discouragement and frustration with procedures that do not promote effective teaching strategies and do not support students in ways that promote mastery or consider all domains of the developing child. Teachers identify these changes as a loss for themselves and their students. They also feel resigned about the changes that are in place. They feel they are no longer heard in their profession. Teachers describe reform changes as "now the bottom line" with no power or authority to alter its course.

4

State Tests and Their Power in the Classroom

The intentions of the early reform movement were to improve the standards of learning for American students. No Child Left Behind (NCLB) uses test results and mandated accountability systems to monitor our nation's school progress in that effort. Test scores define success or failure for schools and they measure the work of classroom teachers. They also determine the ultimate success or failure of this sweeping reform plan. In compliance with federal guidelines, states have designed standardized tests to determine high-stakes decisions including school adequacy, whether or not students will pass to a next grade or graduate, and which teachers will be recognized as competent or in need of focused supervision. The power and effects of high-stakes test scores on the education process are the focus of this chapter. We will examine how NCLB standardized testing policy has changed the meaning of state assessments and how teachers are responding to the pressures of producing high test scores.

NCLB provides us with a framework of monitoring student achievement that sets a new tone of accountability and consequences in public education. Unlike earlier reform efforts, this one includes an undercurrent of sanctions, penalties, and disciplinary actions that clearly influence compliance. The guidelines are very specific. Following state curriculum standards, states are required to set measurable yearly goals for students establishing the 2001–2002 school year as a baseline or starting point. They are required to set up a uniform testing system that measures and tracks the progress of all students in grades 3–8 in math and English to ensure that "adequate yearly progress" (AYP) is made through the continuum of skills. By 12th grade, all students are expected to reach the level of state-defined proficiency in math and reading. Science assessments are to be added in 2007–2008. In addition, states are required to administer state-level assessments based on the state's curriculum standards. A percentage of students from each state is also required to participate in the National Assessment of Education Progress (NAEP) reading and math tests in grades 4 and 8. Often referred to as the "nation's report card," this test provides a curriculum standard that all states are measured against. This test is an equalizer confirming the same expectations for all students.

The American public supports standardized testing. In a 2002 survey by Educational Testing Service, 73% of adults favored testing student achievement and holding teachers and school districts responsible for outcomes. Teachers also support the use of standardized tests as one indicator of progress. Seventy-three percent of teachers polled by Public Agenda (2001) strongly or somewhat agreed that "standardized tests can motivate kids and diagnose problems" (p. 1).

All teachers in this study support the use of state assessments but are cautious about the actual purpose of the test and how the information is used.

> Students do not care about tests and make no effort to do well unless they think the scores will count for something so I believe in letting them know that the tests are serious. If the students are really trying, we can get an accurate picture of what we need to do better and where they still need help. (09-14-27)

Using test results to guide curriculum decisions is sound educational practice and teachers agreed that current state tests can be informative in this regard. They also recognized the limitations of one test score:

> Standardized tests tell us how students are doing in a general sense and I support that but they can't give us a true picture of yearly progress. There are so many factors that indicate the progress a child has made in the course of a year. In our district, we teach with the thought of meeting the needs of the whole child. I don't know how a standardized test can measure that but that doesn't mean it is less important than math and reading scores. (09-12-32)

RELIABILITY AND VALIDITY OF STANDARDIZED TESTS

There is nothing magical about standardized tests. Whether they are designed to measure students against national norms or they are designed to test students on a set body of knowledge, standardized tests can only give us information on the information they are designed to measure. As we consider the high stakes attached to the role of testing in NCLB, it is worthwhile to examine the validity and reliability of standardized tests.

The reliability of a test tells us that we can be confident that tests results are accurate and information from one set of test scores can be compared to another set of test scores. Following current accountability criteria, we would want to be reasonably certain that scores from one district could be compared to another district. Several factors can compromise the reliability of test scores. Comparing groups from year to year has doubtful reliability because of the large variations that can occur in school populations from one year to the next. The level of diversity and school size can also affect the reliability of test scores. Issues of poverty, poor health care, and transitory populations as well as the low numbers of students in small schools are all factors that skew scores. Recent studies in Massachusetts, Florida, and Maine show a majority of schools having high gains in scores one year only to drop the following year. Researchers attribute this confusing pattern to "random fluctuations" due to natural variations in population changes and simple statistical error (Figlio, 2002; Lee, 2002; Mathis, 2003). Comparing populations with these kinds of variations is difficult and, if it is to be done accurately, requires informed interpretation of test scores.

Test validity rests on the reasonable assurance that the test in question is based on material that was actually taught. In order for state assessments to provide a true picture of successful understanding of state standards, the curriculum and the state tests must be aligned. In a study done by the American Federation of Teachers (AFT) in 2001, it was found that 44% of the state tests did not align with state curriculum standards. In the same study, the AFT found that less than a third of state assessments were supported by curriculum that could deliver the results the state was looking for. Additionally, most state assessments focus on math and English, resulting in a limited interpretation of a student's actual academic gains in a school year. The credibility of test results must be considered carefully when test reliability and validity are in question.

Teachers in this study described challenges they have faced as they tried to meet state and local expectations that were not consistent:

> The fact that we don't know what the state test will want and we are teaching kids with a set of district goals that are different makes it very hard to meet everyone's goals for us as teachers. We don't have a look at what the state wants. There have been writing assessments on the test that we didn't understand not to mention the kids. In contrast, we use a writing assessment in our district that really reflects our teaching of the six traits of writing. Students are more likely to be invested in an assessment if it really reflects the material they have studied rather than arbitrarily filling in the dots. They are applying concepts they have been taught. Isn't that the idea behind testing? (05-03-04)

A high school teacher from a "high scoring" district commented on the lack of communication between the state, her district, and her building:

> I have attended every workshop the state has offered in my area to get a clear understanding of what the test is looking for. My students have always done well on tests but I wanted to be sure I was doing what the state wanted. As we were approaching test time, the district came out with all of these guidelines to follow to prepare the kids. I followed those, too. Because this is a new test this year, I think everybody was just guessing because it turned out that the test didn't follow the information I was given. I was very frustrated and so were my students. The test didn't reflect our teaching. We were not properly informed and I am angry about that. (12-01-15)

For other districts, the issue of alignment came down to available staff or budget to rewrite the curriculum to match the state standards. A teacher from an inner-city school explained:

> The state standards are fine and we can support them. Our problem is that we just don't have the staff development time to take our current curriculum and rewrite it to match those standards. It is that simple. So teachers look at the standards and do their best to match them. We do a lot of drilling around test time. (04-12-06)

In addition to not aligning the state test with the district curriculum, teachers expressed a growing concern that scores did not offer a true assessment of what students did know:

> The problem is that the material keeps expanding and the testing services can't keep up with it. They also can't possibly cover everything we teach. For example, take the topic of genetics. They choose a couple of questions from the vast knowledge we have on genetics and think they can tell us if we are doing a good job of teaching that topic. In reality, all you know is how many kids got that one question right. (04-14-12)

TEST PREPARATION

In response to the pressures of high-stakes testing, school districts require teachers to allocate classroom time specifically to test preparation. Of the 180 days or 36 weeks of the instructional year, teachers in this study reported dedicating 12 to 15 weeks of their teaching time to test preparation, test taking, and related activities. This is a range of 33% to 40% of the teaching year! Teachers in this study feel test preparation procedure has no lasting value in the learning process and is simply a concession to political pressures outside of the classroom. They resent this intrusion on their instructional time, which they have already described as too limited. They also believe it compromises information teachers could use to improve instruction.

Teachers talked about how test samples were used before the testing day:

> They give us a common item. They say, "This is an example of what a test question is going to look like." Then we run those common items and put them on overheads for the kids and we practice that process so that when kids see it on the test, they recognize the methods, the vocabulary, and the way to answer. We have to walk them through the process over and over again. It takes so much time. In the end, some of them get it. (10-1-66)

Another teacher describes how time is taken away from regular instruction to practice test format strategies:

> We have to start preparing our students eight weeks in advance of the test. It is the biggest waste of my time. I already know my kids are prepared. And

I know they are going to do just fine. But because our district is very scared of what parents think we are given these pretests that we had to give the kids with questions that they think will be on the test. So I lose three 45-minute classes for that! That is minimal compared to what is going on in other districts. It is ridiculous. (12-04-28)

In addition to lost instructional time, teachers lose valuable planning time:

After we spend time testing our students, we have to sit down in our departments and figure out which ones the kids missed and bring that back to the classroom to teach from. I'm not certain what purpose that serves because we don't even know what is going to be on the test. We don't know the main focus. (11-04-11)

Time once spent on instruction is now reallocated to practice-test taking and familiarizing students with its procedure. In these illustrated cases, actual student knowledge is not expanded by teacher instruction. In some cases, preparing for test procedures actually decreases student understanding of the complexities of their curriculum. Teachers recognize that valuable teaching time is lost in test preparation efforts.

Research suggests that high-stakes standardized testing places profound pressure on teachers to either teach test preparation or risk negative public scrutiny. In an observational study of standardized test effects on instructional practices of Arizona elementary teachers, Smith (1991) finds that making results public "initially produced teacher anxiety, shame, loss of esteem, and alienation" (p. 9). Teachers focused their energies on doing whatever it took to raise test scores. Content was narrowed and teaching strategies were simplified. Computational skills replaced problem-solving skills and simple punctuation replaced writing and language skills. Teaching became test-like in approach and students were trained to search for one right answer rather than think critically.

A high school teacher in this study supported Smith's findings:

I used to teach students to look at problems from different angles. This is common in science. But now I teach them the facts because that is what they need for the test. More and more, teachers in my department are saying if it's not on the test, don't waste the time teaching it. Students have to think in a way that is consistent with what the test is looking for. (01-2-10)

In contrast, teachers support testing for proficiency when it follows instruction based on the actual curriculum:

We have writing standards that we teach in our district. All students learn the format that we expect them to follow. This instruction begins in elementary school and continues through the middle school and on into the high school. All kids understand the terms and work through levels of practice to write according to these standards. I don't think this is teaching to a test. This is teaching an established curriculum and then testing students on their proficiency. These skills are important. (20-1-03)

Professional ethics are also questioned by teachers as they give clear examples of test score pollution and population manipulation to artificially raise test score averages in some districts.

Some districts are, all of a sudden, doing very well on the state tests. I know we have changed and I don't like it. Now we are saying if it's not on the test, we don't teach it. Also there are different levels on the test booklets. I know some teachers look at those levels and think about which kids will get which tests to improve class averages. I know that is awful to say, but I know some districts are under terrible pressure to look good and they are going to do whatever it takes to make an 85% mastery rate for their schools. (10-3-37)

Teachers in this study resented these tactics. At the same time, they described their own efforts to impress upon students a sense of pressure to "do their best" on tests in ways that created serious strain for some students and alienated some parents.

Reform pressures have led to questionable preparation and test-taking practices around the country. While debate continues over the ethics behind student preparation, scholars make three concluding points about the reality of current standardized testing practices: (a) test pollution practices are a reality and they are widespread, (b) score comparisons are not reliable when some districts have the resources to use extensive test preparation practices and others do not, and (c) score pollution can raise students' scores without increasing achievement (Cohn, Kottkamp, & Provenzo, 1987).

THE UNPREDICTABILITY OF STUDENT PERFORMANCE

The impact of test scores varies to some degree between states. In some states, the tests are tied into grade promotion or graduation and carry significant pressure on students to do well. In other states, scores have no direct impact on students. In either case, the scores are considered a measure of teacher competency and school accountability.

Teachers in this study discussed how students' perceptions of the test affect their performance:

> The test in our state has no influence whatsoever on the students. Therefore, they approach the test very differently than they would the SATs, where their future is at stake. The test doesn't count toward grades or promotion. I find it very interesting that they are saying the kids are doing so poorly on the state test, but the SAT scores are going up every year. So to me that indicates the students aren't taking the test seriously. They couldn't care less about what they get. The problem is that the scores do reflect back on our school. Teachers are held accountable. I think eventually it will have to be geared toward graduation. If you ask kids, they'll say, "I don't care what I get on it." (01-2-2)

An elementary teacher also shared concerns about students who didn't "do their best" on the test. She described "threatening" students as a way to promote better student performance on her level:

> Well, in elementary school, they still care about test scores. You know, they ask me if they will still pass if they don't do well on the test and I tell them it doesn't mean anything. But then I wonder, maybe I should say "Yes, it does have something to do with passing." Maybe then they would do their best. Like older kids, we are finding that some just go A, B, C, D, right down the line and not even read the questions! So I am not bothered with threatening for results. It might mean they will try harder. (10-1-119)

While motivating disinterested students to test well can be helpful to schools, these same efforts can cause serious stresses for other students. In these cases, teachers' efforts can strain students and parents:

> Parent: It was all of the commotion they made about the test at school. The teachers were really hyped about them, you know, telling kids for weeks ahead of the time that they have to know this or that for the test. If they

didn't get it, they would do bad on the test. If they didn't pay attention the whole school would look bad for the test. I'm not kidding, Allison was worrying about the test for weeks before she even took it! By the time they were taking the test, she wasn't sleeping at night. She was just a wreck!

Interviewer: What did you tell her?

Parent: We told her it wasn't a big deal but it wasn't us she was worried about. She said they told the kids that if one of them doesn't pay attention, it can hurt the whole class's score. Of course, Allison starts worrying about the class average. She thought if she missed something, the whole class would be mad at her. I think the teachers are as much of a wreck about the test as the kids. (13-1-14, 18, 25)

In a similar conversation, a middle school parent felt teachers were responsible for too much pressure on students:

I don't know what is going on up at that school. John has never reacted to tests like this before. For weeks ahead of the day all he did was talk about how important the score was and that the class would be responsible for the results. The teachers were on them all of the time practicing for the test and he was having trouble sleeping he got so worried. I don't know where it is coming from but I don't like teachers putting this kind of pressure on kids. (13-2-4)

The pressure to generate high test scores is seen in the ways teachers react to students' attitudes about the test. Teachers describe how unreliable students force them to approach students in ways that could maximize student performance. The cost of these efforts is seen in strained relationships with students and parents who do not understand or appreciate the pressure behind teachers' efforts to produce high test scores. Resulting tensions between teachers, parents, and students produce further frustrations for teachers, who feel compelled to produce high scores.

STATE ASSESSMENTS AND COMMUNITY ENFORCEMENT: THE TYRANNY OF PUBLIC DISCLOSURE

Mandated public disclosure of state assessment scores is a powerful enforcer of the national reform plan. Disclosure ensures statewide awareness of individual school progress toward reform goals. Reports based on one state test score are released yearly to districts and their communities by the state education agencies. Additionally, the test scores are released to state newspapers as well as television and radio stations for public broadcast. Information is generally organized to provide average scores of each grade level. The format easily allows the reader to compare all schools within a district and also compare districts throughout the state. Districts can be identified on a continuum of highest achievement to lowest achievement.

Public disclosure of test scores is a heated topic for teachers. For many, the competition between schools is seen as unfair and inaccurate when considering the realities of the school year. Variables that cannot be controlled such as student diversity, family mobility, tax bases, and shifting resources all contribute to what a school can and cannot do. Adding in the emotional and social stigmas of being associated with low-scoring or "failing" schools compounds the burden for teachers, students, families, and neighborhoods in significant ways.

A teacher who works in a high-scoring district but lives in a low-scoring district supports published test scores:

> The district I live in isn't scoring well. I am very angry for my children because I see what other children do in high-scoring districts. My thinking is if publishing test scores forces teachers to look at their curriculum and change their scores, then publish the test scores. That's not a bad thing. So I guess I am looking at the ends justifying the means in this respect. It is the only leverage that I see parents having to hold schools accountable. (3-93-107)

A high school teacher from a high-scoring district saw low-scoring schools as having more obstacles to overcome before they can try to compete with other schools:

> Well, I teach here so I think "go for it," because I am very proud of test scores. We do very, very well here. But we also work with really good kids. Part of me thinks the other schools' scores should be published because they should be held accountable but then another part of me says I don't know. It's not fair for the schools that have so much going against them before the kids even get to school. (12-04-30)

Teachers saw the current system of relying on one test score to determine competence as providing the public with a very limited view of what they do. They argued for examination of more complete data to assess a school's successes or failures:

> You can't just look at test scores when you are deciding if a school is failing. You have to look at other factors like drop-out rates and successful completion of a school year. And then analyze data and start with kindergarten. Education is in turmoil and it needs help. But you have to take the time to do some data collecting and find out the trends before you decide whether or not a school is failing. If you take a wealthy community against a poor community, there is no way that you can discount parent education and income. You can't discount teachers. Most teachers want to live in communities that provide a higher standard of living. They are educated people and want access to cultural life. They want to be close to cities rather than rural communities. It is a vicious circle. Poor places have less resources and less to offer talented people who have choices. There is plenty of data telling us that schools are failing but unless we are looking at the whole picture and finding out why, we are never going to change anything. (03-432-28)

Districts that have the money, staff, and resources to successfully adopt the state standards into school curriculum score much better than those districts that do not. The comparison shifts from teacher quality to economic realities for many schools. Organizing schools by test scores also creates a labeling or categorizing of schools that isn't always fair or accurate:

> In districts that have less resources like some of the poorer towns, people will read those test scores and say, "My kids are going to a bad school so I am going to switch to another school." Or, if they can, they move out of the community. Those who don't have those options feel like they are stuck with "bad" schools and "bad" teachers." That affects how kids feel about their school and how teachers feel working there. (09-2-10)

> I don't think you can help but look at the test scores and you say, well, this really benefited the wealthy districts and hurts the poor ones. It supports an arrogance for the one that scores well and it creates a self-defeating cycle for the other. It's really not good for anybody. It becomes an issue of total competition rather than cooperation to include everyone or work together. It's who can do better, get better, is better. (09-2-12)

Schools labeled as "failing" face declining enrollment and decreased funding. The result is a neighborhood school that cannot attract strong teachers or maintain parent commitment.

> As a parent, I wouldn't want my child in a school that people were exiting. And if people have the choice to go to a different school then you are going to end up with a school full of kids whose parents don't have the resources or power to make different choices. I know what a school looks like with a bad reputation. You can't attract staff. Morale is terrible. Kids give up. It is important to force a struggling school to look at itself. Bringing in mentors and partnering with sister schools helps. But creating divisions and labeling schools can only hurt the kids who already have the most to lose. (03-432-17)

The community experiences a negative ripple effect as schools lose credibility based on low test scores. Students, teachers, and families carry the stigma of a school that has been labeled as failing:

> Parents think you are a bad teacher and your school isn't as good as the neighboring school. They say they are going to do homeschooling or move. People who are thinking about moving into the community, look for homes in other, better scoring communities. Pretty soon scores do a nosedive and then the whole school just starts spiraling down. (09-2-15)

> As horrible as it sounds, schools with low test scores have the kind of kids you don't want your kids associating with. They don't have the kind of motivation you want to see or the economic supports. This is a really snobby thing to say but I don't want my kids to go to a school where the test scores are low. It usually means that you have a bunch of kids who don't care about school and I don't want my kids to run the risk—the big risk—of getting into groups that I don't want them to be with. So as a parent, I will look at those test scores to make those decisions. That isn't the teachers' fault. That isn't even the districts' fault. Schools that don't score well aren't being helped by any of this and it is going to increase class division. (13-07-31)

The pressures of public disclosure also impact building principals in the ways they direct teachers' energies and planning time. One principal I spoke with works in an affluent community. This district has led the state in reform compliance, which has ensured further funding for his school. They enjoy high teacher morale and community endorsement. Homes are expensive and in demand. This school population consistently scores among the top schools on the state assessment.

> It's going to happen whether we like it or not. Our opinion doesn't matter. We really don't have a choice. We can't change it. There are very high expectations from this community. If I am going to be a principal here, I have to understand that parents expect me to have a very good school. And that's how we operate. Kids are kids. Economics make a difference. We have embraced these changes in a positive manner. Some districts have said, "Oh, god, why do we have to do this? The state is making us do this." Our answer has been, "Okay, this is what we're going to do. How do we proceed?" So we are more proactive about change. We are well supported by the community through budget and they expect results. (03-1-92)

This is contrasted with a second principal from a district that scores poorly. They don't have a "well-supported budget" and do not have the resources available to make the changes necessary to raise scores:

> We are vehemently opposed to what is happening with these test results. We are a small school in a small district. We don't have the resources, faculty, or time to rewrite our curriculum to fit the state tests. Our kids have too many other issues that deserve our attention and focus. Nobody wants to talk about those issues, though, and nobody wants to fund them enough to change them. (12-1-3)

When resources are limited and community support is weak, districts have to make hard choices. The community interprets poor scores as poor teaching. Should they focus teacher time on the immediate needs of students or on meeting requirements of the state test? For some schools, a disproportionate "at-risk" population and poor test scores jeopardize an already strained school budget. Additionally, not rewriting curriculum to meet state frameworks has resulted in denied state and federal funding. Under new NCLB guidelines, this school will be facing increased sanctions and the added costs of parent choice, busing, and tutorial programming for failing students.

> Oh, it's all wrong. You take kids from a wealthy community who might have average teachers and strong family experiences with preschool from age two and they are probably going to score well. You take a poor community where

unemployment is high and the average education of parents is low and these kids are beat before they start. They can have the best teachers in the state — it doesn't change the fact that they are behind before they start the first day of school. You can't use raw scores to determine which district is doing the best work. These assessments are only one tool. (07-1-19)

A teacher who was a union liaison for her district summarized what teachers thought in her district:

Under NCLB guidelines, test scores drive everything. But we are comparing apples to oranges and most people don't understand that. You are comparing kids from one year to a different group of kids the next year. Even when they are monitoring the same cohort, the actual populations change, especially in poor communities. You are talking about comparing districts with lots of money and parent support to districts with no resources and then saying the teachers are accountable. (03-24-48)

The results of relying on test scores to compare and evaluate schools are significant. Districts have a powerful incentive to write standardized curriculum to match the state test. At the same time, public understanding of actual school effectiveness or teacher effort is narrowed. Disparate local funding traditions and shifting school populations prohibit an equal opportunity for districts to respond to change initiatives. Teachers wrestle with precarious public perceptions of their work in this storm of fiscal inequality, student unpredictability, and limited understanding and analysis of test meanings. Schools are left with the sole option of finding better ways to incorporate curriculum standards and improve test results or lose all hope of maintaining community support. It isn't surprising that strong teachers and administrators leave for friendlier, more successful districts.

GRADE PROMOTION AND GRADUATION STANDARDS

Supporters of graduation or "exit" tests contend that it is not unreasonable to expect all students to demonstrate a level of proficiency in certain skills before they pass between grades or graduate from high school. The discussion of exit tests becomes more heated as we define the weight of these tests, who should be taking them, and if they should be the only determining measurement for advancement.

A survey conducted by Business Roundtable in August 2000 found three-quarters of parents and nonparents agreed that children should have to pass reading and math tests to be promoted from fourth grade even if they have passing grades in all their classes (Belden, Russonello, & Stewart Firm, 2000a). Eighty-eight percent of the teachers in a study for *Education Week* supported end-of-the-year tests but only when used along with other considerations including grades, developmental and social maturity, and supporting assessment data (Belden, Russonello, & Stewart Firm, 2000b).

An elementary teacher explained her concerns:

> One test is completely unfair for anyone and certainly not a reliable indicator for elementary-age students. They aren't good at pressure to begin with plus anything can upset them to the point where they can't concentrate and perform. Common sense tells us to look at their overall performance for an entire year and then you have to consider the effects of retention on the whole child, not just the child in relationship to reading or math. (02-13-27)

Secondary teachers support the use of high-stakes testing more than elementary teachers. In the same study done by *Education Week*, 37% supported the use of exit exams to graduate and 58% of the teachers supported exit exams when used with other academic records (Belden, Russonello, & Stewart Firm, 2000b). Teachers saw value in working toward a test to indicate competence or completion. They agreed that students study harder and pay more attention if they know they will have to pass a test to be promoted or to graduate. High school teachers who work in states with graduation tests feel academic standards make their curriculum more demanding, raise their own expectations on what they want students to achieve, and believe their own students work harder and learned more. They also feel they spend too much time on tests at the cost of less teaching time (Belden, Russonello, & Stewart Firm, 2000b).

High school teachers discussed the added problem of students who just aren't motivated and parents who don't support school efforts:

> I do not think you should pass kids who have not mastered grade-level work. This is a big problem in education. When they say every child will succeed what do they mean? I tend to lean toward the hard line. We let kids get away with too much. Teachers are passing kids who just shouldn't be passed. It is just easier to pass them. There is only so much hounding you can do and only so many times you can call home. So I understand why teachers give up and

just pass them. I also see the other side, that some kids just don't give a rip
about school or what good is retaining him going to do? So I don't know how
to solve that issue. There is retention that will help some kids and there is retention that isn't going to do any good at all. (12-04-19)

On the other side of this issue is the reality that high-stakes testing
holds serious consequences for students who do not score well.

If we are going to keep raising the bar it is going to mean that more kids will
not meet the standards. I don't really have a problem with raising standards
but what is going to happen to those kids? Do they just not graduate? Do
they drop out? We don't offer an alternative program or other options. Our
district has no plan except to have them repeat curriculum. (12-13-17)

At-risk kids are impacted the most by these aggressive sanctions. They
don't have the support system outside of school that could help them so we
"up" the level of expectations; we also up the risks for them. (03-43-18)

A serious challenge to the success of NCLB is recognizing and addressing the many reasons that students fail. We know that most students
who drop out of school share similar disadvantages, including poverty,
poorly educated parents, inadequate health care, and minimal parent involvement with the school. We know these children come to school behind more advantaged children and that their chances to overcome those
differences are not good. Many of these students need more time to learn
than we currently provide in our age-graded system. Many have learning
differences, speak a different language, or just don't test well. They tend
to change schools more often and they have fewer connections in the community. We know these children are more expensive to educate.

Teachers described the effects of family struggles on children and the
resulting emotional issues that limited achievement for some students:

Test scores are one measure of how well you taught. They do reflect how
well you teach in one respect. But then, again, a lot depends on the student
and family. You can give me the best student with family issues and I'm still
not going to bring that child to a level like a child coming from a supportive home. So there are too many factors we have no control over. I guess
that is why we feel so vulnerable. (03-3-54)

The emotional problems are so serious. There is so much abuse and chemical and alcohol problems. Many days, kids come here and I can't expect a day's work from them. They are in too much pain. The effects of what is happening at home are too much for them. It is remarkable that they even got here sometimes. You can see it in their eyes. The pain is swirling around. These kids can hardly sit in a chair. They aren't going to care about multiplication facts. They need to be verbal. They need to block out the noises in their heads. They need a place to work out what has hurt them. All of that has to happen before they can settle down and learn. Sometimes it takes days or even weeks to work through that stuff. In the meantime, we are racing through curriculum to get to the tests. (11-1-8, 16)

Teachers argue that teaching and learning do not occur in a vacuum. The classroom is a highly dynamic and complex environment. Students come to school with significant differences in prior knowledge, cognitive abilities, social-emotional development, and linguistic experiences. Teachers feel addressing these issues is a critical component in their work. When differences are not addressed the opportunities to learn are diminished. Tensions often develop in the classroom and students begin acting out in negative ways, fall into apathy, or drop out of school. Despite significant research that links learning to developmental stages and emotional climate in the classroom, the reform efforts continue on a narrowing path that limits teachers' time, authority, and expertise to address these issues in the classroom.

As a nation, we do not fund schools equally. We provide the fewest resources to the schools with the greatest needs. The differences in per-pupil expenditures, resource materials, and the upkeep of facilities between high- and low-income communities are staggering. These schools also have the hardest time attracting and keeping strong teachers and administrators. Salaries tend to be lower and the working conditions tend to be more demanding with fewer supports. These communities do not have property values that generate taxes to support school improvements and parents don't have the incomes to subsidize school programs. As we look at the promise of NCLB, we have to consider how we can expect every child to pass the same test when we continue to disregard the effects of poverty and school funding discrepancies.

High-stakes testing results in winners and losers. Students who feel that school is a futile effort are more likely to drop out. *Education Week* reported in 2002 that students who had to pass eighth-grade tests were more likely to drop out of high school by tenth grade (Viadero, 2003). This was confirmed in a study by Berliner and Amrein, who studied graduation rates of 16 of the 18 states requiring students to pass graduation exams. They found that dropout rates increased in most of the states (Viadero, 2003). Currently, 27 states have established graduation policies that include exit exams and 18 require students to pass a test even if they have passing grades in all subject (Schouten, 2003). It is interesting to note that current federal guidelines require states to report the number of dropouts but the information is not factored into accountability assessments. This irony may be driving scores up but at the cost of pushing more students out of the system. Teachers are in agreement that they do not want to return to lower standards for students who struggle but we may want to consider what we are doing to the students who can't reach them.

COSTS AND CONSIDERATIONS OF TESTING

State and federal budget cuts are colliding with the escalating costs of annual testing with no end in sight. The Bush administration has proposed $100 million to help states write and administer tests in the early years of implementation. According to Achieve, a Cambridge, Massachusetts, nonprofit group, state testing expenditures have tripled to over $390 million in the past five years and the costs are climbing. Not surprisingly, trends in testing have shifted from an emphasis on performance such as oral reports, demonstrations, or essays, to a multiple choice format. They are much easier to administer and score, they cost less, averaging about $17.50 per test in 1998 dollars compared to as much as $100.00 per test for performance-based tests, and they are relatively easy to align with state standards (Olson, 2001).

Teachers question multiple choice tests when the stakes to prove achievement and competency are so high. Critics of multiple choice formats contend that multiple-choice tests can only address lower-order thinking skills and the addition of some short answer questions or writing samples do not offer a true picture of what students can do.

> How can you seriously think that a multiple-choice test is going to show you any depth of student achievement? I have students who are great at analyz-

ing data and thinking in terms of social trends and development. That can't be measured on a multiple-choice test. You really have to let them write an essay, analyze a short story, or look at a portfolio to see proof of those skills. Then you can tell me if I have taught what was needed. (05-03-27)

NATIONAL OBSERVATIONS

Education scholars have described the consequences of the pressures generated from standardized testing as profoundly seen in the work of classroom teachers (Koretz, Madaus, Haertel, & Beaton, 1992). Berliner and Biddle characterize assessment scores as a "carrot and stick" approach to accountability (1995). They identify standardized assessment as focusing on extrinsic sanctions—the contingent application of rewards or punishment by others. Researchers have concluded teachers respond poorly to such sanctions and the effects are seen in their work. Smith (1991) finds that over time teachers' curricula and teaching efforts became more standardized and monitored. Deci and Ryan (1982) conclude that standardized multiple-choice tests force teachers to focus on broad, superficial converge. Berliner and Biddle (1995) see course content "covered at a 'gallop,' foreswearing the time that might be 'wasted' on encouraging reasoning, student thoughtfulness, or application to course content" (p. 195). Researchers confirmed what teachers have reported. In efforts to help their schools "look good" to the public, teachers are restricting instruction to only those topics assessed by the tests (Gillman & Reynolds, 1991; Wirth, 1992).

In a study done by Gilles, Gelleta, and Daniels in Missouri (1994), standardized tests were tied to a new curriculum. The scores were then used in a state "report card" to let the public know how schools compared statewide:

> The results of this program were most alarming. Quality programs and textbooks were scrapped in order to replace them with materials that directly taught the test and an unholy competition emerged between districts and communities over test scores. In some districts a week or more of instructional time each year was devoted to preparing for this test. (p. 1)

Additionally, there is growing evidence of districts cheating to enhance test scores. Examples included distribution of test questions prior to the testing day, teaching only restricted curricula that aligned directly with the test or exempting low-achieving students from the testing population, which resulted in inflated test scores (National Commission on Testing and Public Policy, 1990). Results of these practices seriously impacted test integrity and strained professional ethics for teachers.

Education scholars of assessment standards and teachers in this study argue the fact that schools do not start from a "level playing field" in standardized testing requirements. Researchers document that our schools exhibit great extremes of wealth and poverty (Apple, 1990; Berliner & Biddle, 1995; Cohn & Kottkamp, 1993). The National Center for Education Statistics (1997) reports that schools serving impoverished students have a fraction of the funds given to public schools in wealthier communities. Poorly supported schools are also the schools most likely to "lose" in accountability contests.

In a recent nationwide survey, Americans also expressed growing dissatisfaction with some components of NCLB. According to the 37th Annual Phi Delta Kappa/Gallup Polls of the *Public's Attitudes toward the Public Schools* released in 2005, 68% of the public do not agree that one test score can give an accurate appraisal of a school (Gallup & Rose, 2005). Eighty percent of the public also feel that testing only math and English provides insufficient information to label a school as needing improvement. While the public supports testing, they are at least as likely to blame the way NCLB mandates acceptable progress as they are to blame their schools for poor performance. These results suggest a shift in public attitudes toward a more reasoned and expanded approach to evaluating schools and their teachers. It might be a good time for policy makers to note these changes.

STATE TEST SCORES AND THEIR POWER IN THE CLASSROOM

Teachers, parents, and government leaders agree that standardized testing is important in the evaluation of student progress and the assessment of curriculum and instructional strategies. This chapter has examined how high-stakes testing has changed the way teachers interpret and approach testing in their classrooms. We have looked at how these tests are affecting students and their communities. We have extended this information to include national studies considering similar issues. Teachers in this study have provided sobering insights into what they are seeing as these tests gain increasing power over their work.

Teachers describe hours of teaching time now devoted specifically to preparing students for the assessments and its format. Teachers agree that these efforts do nothing to increase student knowledge and the resulting scores are limited indicators of actual student achievement. They do not support this use of their time. Professional ethics are also questioned by teachers as they relate examples of test score pollution and population manipulation to artificially raise student test score averages in some districts. Teachers resent these tactics. At the same time, they describe their own efforts to impress upon students a sense of pressure to "do their best" on tests in ways that create strain for some students and alienate some parents.

The marginal understanding of the facts and circumstances behind published test scores also holds serious consequences for students, neighborhood schools, and for teachers. Current practices of comparing high-achieving districts to low-achieving districts are unfair and misleading when they fail to describe the effects of inequities that teachers and schools cannot control. These scores take on added significance as generalizations spill over into stigmas about the people who live in those communities and teachers who work in their schools.

> Teachers do feel vulnerable. Part of it comes from what is really hard to measure—what we do and how successful we are. I've had years where my test scores were off the wall and they were wonderful and I know it wasn't just because of me. It was because I had wonderful students. I've had other years where I had to work harder than I have ever worked before and my test scores are lower. Only because that was the population I had. I think that's part of it. It's hard to prove how good we are. (03-3-52)

Teachers support the use of standards as a gauge for passing students into higher grades and for graduation. They do not support basing these important decisions on one test score. Similarly, they see serious consequences in a testing system that creates winners and losers. Raising standards carries the added responsibility of seeing to the needs of students who need extra help and added supports to achieve those goals. There is consensus among teachers that more time and effort must be directed to finding solutions to these serious problems.

On its current path, the reform movement is riveted on achievement outcomes. Incomplete interpretations of the scores are seen by the public and education authorities as a reflection on teacher competence rather than a statement about test validity and an understanding of the population it has measured. In a system that quantifies student success by a single yearly score, teachers are left in the very vulnerable position of being responsible for working with qualitative variables they often can't predict or control. The next chapter looks at how teachers' relationships with their students are shifting as a result of the precarious link between high-stakes testing and teacher accountability.

III

Changes in Teachers' Perceptions About Their Profession and Their Responsibilities

5

Teachers and Their Students

The relations between students and their teachers are complicated and very difficult to measure or assess. We do know students who like their teachers do better in school. Most of us can name our own favorite teacher with little prompting. When asked to explain why one teacher stands out from the others, we can generally come up with qualities that separated a favorite teacher from others such as "she was interesting," "the classes were inspiring," "he was enthusiastic," or simply, "she cared about me." These descriptions led to a sense of being connected to the teacher, learning seemed more meaningful, and we remember feelings of success.

Teachers also speak candidly about the importance of their relationships with students. They agree that there is no way to measure this influence but they recognize its importance in their classrooms. The No Child Left Behind (NCLB) Strategic Plan Handbook also recognizes the impact of the relationship between students and their teachers:

> While research has shown that a few measurable attributes relate to student achievement—such as master's degrees in math or science or teachers' verbal ability—more than 90% of a teacher's influence on student achievement goes unexplained. (U.S. Department of Education, 2002, p. 41)

In this chapter, we will examine the relational connection between teachers and students and the changes teachers are seeing as NCLB is implemented in the classroom.

ALIGNING TEACHER QUALITY WITH STUDENT TEST SCORES

While the NCLB handbook acknowledges that more than 90% of a teacher's influence on achievement cannot be explained, the law relies on the remaining 10% to determine teacher quality. The handbook goes on to explain:

> We know from research that improving teacher and principal quality will lead to improved achievement, though we also know that measuring "teacher quality" or "principal quality" is very difficult. So the best performance measure for this objective is student achievement, as expressed in the indicators for objectives 2.1, 2.2, and 2.3 (achievement on national and state assessments in reading, mathematics, and science, disaggregated by subgroups). (p. 41)

It is here that we begin to see the effects of NCLB implementation. As teachers work to follow the curriculum guidelines and assessment timelines, they describe changes in how they are approaching their students:

> It's like you have to create robots in learning and you are discouraging the naturalness of children. So it's not the whole child we are looking at. It's the intellectual child. But the emotional, spiritual, physical part of this has dropped off . . . almost like we are going to create mutants. (09-2-06)

Teachers describe their students as complex human beings with many needs. They feel an important part of their work is to understand and address emotional and social needs of the students before learning can occur. They recognize this part of teaching as very time consuming but also very meaningful:

> We have lots and lots of kids who come to school with too much emotional baggage and they come with academic needs that students didn't have before. We have to deal with that because if they can't function, it affects everyone else's opportunity to learn. They react by being disruptive. Other times, they will just withdraw and that won't affect the rest of the kids, but it will affect the child and me. I can't handle knowing that child isn't learning. I have to find ways to help that child. And a child who really acts out or is withdrawn is very time consuming . . . extremely time consuming if that is going to be turned around. I can't ignore that. I have had a lot of success with those kids . . . and it is very rewarding. (11-1-6)

Teachers speak of the escalating number of students who come to school with severe social and emotional needs. Many times their families struggle with poverty, chemical and drug abuse, emotional illness, and domestic violence. When these children come to school, they bring these complex family problems with them. Teachers speak of emotional and behavioral control issues so pressing that nothing can be accomplished until they are resolved. The problems increase with the size and complexity of the school. Outsiders or people who do not deal directly with students do not understand the time required for teachers to restore and maintain classroom control.

Similar concerns are ways that time restrictions and curriculum controls limit attention to the different developmental stages of children. One teacher talked about the importance of "exploration time" for younger children:

> We have no time for inspiration in the learning process anymore. We never give kids the opportunity to explore and to learn and to develop those skills and assist it. So we'll look at the year's curriculum and say it looks good on paper, but they are six- or seven-year-olds. Play is an important part of learning and we need to allow time for that. You can't structure every minute for them and no longer allow them to explore. They are six years old! (03-3-85)

Education researchers Cohn and Kottkamp produced national findings in 1993 that were consistent with concerns of teachers in this study. Ninety-five percent of teachers they surveyed expressed their purpose as being more than teaching academic contents. The teachers stressed the importance of identifying and teaching to all developmental sides of a child. Learning from this perspective goes well beyond results on a standardized test. It considers the cultural, moral, social, and emotional sides of a child in addition to the measurement of academic achievements. The combination of these profiles contributes to understanding the relationships effective teachers have with their students. As teachers work to meet curriculum objectives and follow test deadlines, the opportunities that were once available for interaction with students and their development stages outside the academic setting are often compromised or completely ignored. Teachers resort to instruction that has a single focus and one right answer. There is no real need for interpersonal relationships in this teaching format and individuality has less significance (Cohn & Kottkamp, 1993).

With increased pressures to meet test deadlines, teachers also acknowledge that they prefer to limit their classrooms to students who are "nice kids, respectful and hardworking" as opposed to students who might need adaptations to the curriculum, complain of boredom, or have difficulty keeping up. These students become additional "burdens" in the classroom and can actually create resentment in teachers who struggle to keep the class moving at a specific pace.

The connection between teacher competency and test scores also impacts students' relationship with teachers. Regardless of the reason, students who score poorly on state tests directly impact the perceptions of a teacher's performance and the rankings of the school. It is not surprising that struggling students are increasingly seen as a serious problem in the classroom and to their school.

THE REALITY OF "BELOW GRADE LEVEL" STUDENTS

The standardized curriculum frameworks identify curriculum objectives on a continuum of skills through the grade levels. A basic assumption built into this model is that students achieve mastery of their content curriculum each year. As each new year begins, teachers are responsible for getting students through their own grade level curriculum. Teachers in this study described the reality that students enter each school year with a wide assortment of skills, a broad background of learning experiences, and varying levels of abilities. Standardized yearly curricula do not factor these disparities into expectations of grade-level goals or teacher accountability. This actuality is a serious issue for teachers who are held to timelines that do not include the remediation and review many students require just to catch up with their peers:

> Sometimes you have an entire class that isn't on grade level. Last year, we had one class in this grade like that. The whole class came in under grade level. They were behind before the year even started. It was terrible! The teachers hate it. We are constantly trying to find ways to eliminate that. We do not like sending a child to a next grade who is not on grade level. (11-1-25b)

As students pass through grades, the effects of not being on grade level intensify. A fourth-grade teacher added the observation that many children are developmentally not ready for the expectations in the curriculum frameworks. They need slower instruction and added review, which teachers do not have the time to provide. The result is an increasing number who are not retaining what they are taught:

> Students come to the fourth grade now with a wide range of skills. If we talk to the teachers in the lower grades, they confirm that the material was taught. The students aren't retaining the information from one year to the next. They don't retain basic things they need. So we reteach on the next grade level. Well, by fourth grade there can be a lot of review plus we have all of these new requirements in the frameworks and we have to move so fast to cover it, that the next year teacher also has that to cover with the kids who didn't get it at the speed we were moving the first time. Every level is harder. By sixth grade, it is ridiculous! The teachers are buried. And it all goes back to kids not really having the time to learn the material well in the first place! (11-1-19)

In a frenzy of moving students through the curriculum with decreased teaching time, teachers share a common frustration with students progressing through the grades without adequate remediation or thorough understanding of grade-level material. There aren't many options for schools if students can't stay up with the pace. A high school teacher explained:

> This is an important point because it is like they want it both ways. We might say, "This child isn't ready to go on to the next year." But the district has no power to retain unless the parents agree. So it's like they want it both ways. They want the kids to learn what they need, they want the teachers to be accountable, but we have no recourse if students aren't on grade level at the end of the year. We just keep passing them on. All of a sudden we have tenth graders who are years behind and we say the school isn't meeting expectations. (01-2-82)

An administrator in this district explained the state and district's policy on retention:

> We do not retain kids after the first or second grade unless it is clearly an issue of development. That is to say, the child needs a year of maturing in order to handle grade-level curriculum. Research tells us that retention not only doesn't help kids, it actually hurts them once they get beyond the early years in school. We have supports to help them academically after that. (09-2-4)

Teachers identified the conflict between low-achieving students and no authority to control decisions regarding promotion as a serious one for students and themselves. While the administrator suggested "academic supports" to help failing students, teachers described students as rushed through curriculum, tested before they are ready, and continually pushed to next levels of instruction with little or no added support when it is actually needed. They see instruction in this format as counterproductive to learning. Increased frustrations for teachers and students who are described as problems multiply in higher grades.

> If there was an answer, you would have a lot of very happy teachers. They keep doing all of these studies on retention and say that retention works for a year or two and then it doesn't work anymore. There are alternative schools that are supposed to help but you can't send every kid who isn't on grade level to an alternative school . . . there is just no easy answer. (11-1-25)

CLASSROOM TEACHERS AND THE PRESSURE OF SPECIAL EDUCATION: WE AREN'T FACING THE REAL ISSUES . . .

Students with special needs remain a focus for teachers and district administrators as issues of funding and calls for increased classroom support remain highly political and controversial. According to the National Center for Education Statistics (2002), the number of special education students has nearly doubled since 1977. In the past ten years, the number of special education students has increased at an annual average of 3.2%. Most growth has been in categories that include attention deficit hyperactive disorder (ADHD) and behavioral and emotional disorders.

> The cases we are seeing are definitely becoming more complex. Kids who would never have survived or thrived are surviving with medically complex health issues and we are starting to see them. We have medically fragile kids coming into the system that I am personally afraid of having in the building. I have a master's degree in special education and I have been in the field long enough to know how to do this job. But these kinds of kids just weren't alive when I started teaching. Then we have the parents, who are also under stress trying to work with these disabilities and often can't han-

dle it. The family unit breaks down and that is an added difficulty that we often have to deal with. A lot of our tough cases are from divorced homes, which add a complex piece. And I think parents in general are skeptical about schools. Relationships become adversarial very quickly. (03-432-09)

While debate rages over why the number of special education students continues to grow, educators agree that the greater emphasis on keeping students in school has affected the numbers. Classroom teachers have become better at identifying and referring learning problems in recent years and parents have become more aware of their rights. Educators also agree that the testing requirements of NCLB will fuel this trend. As standards of achievement are raised, the number of students failing will likely increase. Students who may have been passing before will need added supports to meet higher standards. With school budgets already strained, special education is the only source of additional revenues to fund those supports.

The amount of federal dollars allocated for special education has steadily increased. When the original Individuals with Disabilities Act was passed in 1975, it was understood by states that Congress would fund 40% of the national special education costs. Currently, the subsidy is at about 18% with states left to fund the balance. Not surprisingly, how that money is spent is controversial in state-level government and school districts.

The great majority of special education students are mainstreamed into the classroom. Mandated inclusion of special needs students has had a profound impact on teachers. They describe struggles with the growing number of "high need" students and too little time, insufficient resources, and diminished autonomy to answer those needs.

I think it is fine that these kids have exposure to the regular classroom but they need someone to help them and the teacher. You just can't expect the teacher to individualize instruction for every child and redo every test because this kid is dyslexic and this kid can't read and this kid can't write. And you have to think about the disruptions many of these kids cause. If you have an emotionally disturbed child in your classroom and she is disrupting your teaching and you aren't trained to deal with it, you just end up disrupting your class more. More teaching time is lost. Regular students end up sitting there waiting for you to get back to teaching. You can't attend to those kinds of needs when you have a class full of students who are trying to learn a full lesson in 45 minutes. (12-01-17)

Teachers resent the fact that all students are affected when special needs populations are not given adequate support:

> We absolutely do not have the special education support we need. We have support staff and they are extremely dedicated but it's just not enough. For example, in my room I teach fourth grade and I have 30 kids. So many of these kids need support. Out of 30, I have five who are coded and two who are on watch. I have LD [learning disabled] kids and kids on watch for emotional disturbance. They have no services. I have others who don't work unless it is one-on-one. They can't get started on assignments, ever, alone. They have a very low reading level, second grade or less, they receive no special services. There are teachers who have more coded kids than I do. Then there are the kids who will not allow teaching to go on. They are constantly interrupting me and disrupting the students around them. I should have a full-time aide in this classroom but there is no money and no help. (11-2-83)

> We can't get the support we need for these kids. So ALL kids suffer because the child will consume all of the teacher's time just trying to maintain order. Good teachers can do that, but the cost is instruction that isn't done well or other kids' needs never getting addressed. We are mandated to service these kids and I think we should. But no one wants to pay for it so it's the average kids who pay that price. They lose what you would do for them if you could. Right now all we do is plug holes—keep control. We know what these kids need. Everybody knows exactly what needs to be done. But we can't do it. We can't afford those services. So, instead we piecemeal this effort. But it doesn't really work because we aren't facing the real issues. (11-1-17)

For these teachers, the "real issue" of special needs is the lack of special education support for the students who require time-consuming academic and emotional support from their teachers. Without sufficient resources for the mandated students, teacher's energies are put into insufficient "piecemeal efforts" to accommodate special-needs students while taking away time from the regular classroom work teachers feel should be their primary responsibility. Teachers are very frustrated knowing the opportunity to learn is compromised for all students when there is inadequate or nonexistent special-needs support.

Staffing a school with paraprofessionals to help classroom teachers is not easy. The positions tend to be on the low end of the pay scale and the training is often insufficient.

A problem is you get what you pay for. I have a full time para in my room but I might as well be alone. The para is more of a detriment to me than a help. He is a former gym teacher—very brisk and physical with them and a very poor role model. More often than not, I am intervening between him and the child he is supposed to be taking care of because they are fighting and arguing with one another. It's like having another child in the classroom! So on paper I have a full-time aide in the classroom. In reality, I have one more student to deal with. (03-3-64)

A director of special education services in a large district described their training for special education paraprofessionals:

Our aids don't get any training. It is on-the-job training. It is inadequate. This year I have tried to get some people to go to workshops and through their contracts they do get paid for that but you don't get enough. The gamut is so wide. We have some college graduates that haven't gotten a job yet. I hire a ton of them every year knowing that they will last a year. And I have moms who want to get back into the job market. They have no training in education. They desperately need training in behavior management, disabilities that they are dealing with, what to expect, and professionalism. A lot of these people have never worked in an environment where confidentiality and how to work with professionals has ever come up. They feel underappreciated and internalize that resentment. (03-432-29)

NCLB raised the requirements for Title I paraprofessionals to have until January 2006 to either complete two years of college or pass a state or local assessment that demonstrates knowledge and ability to assist students with instruction in reading, writing, or math. Additionally, NCLB provides a list of the types of duties Title I paraprofessionals can perform. The guidelines improve the qualifications of paraprofessionals and provide a better support to special-needs students. Unfortunately, the law does not provide funding for increased salaries, pension, or benefits.

The new law is ridiculous because people are not paid enough. Our aids get paid $9.82 an hour. You can get a job at the mall getting paid more than that. So how can we expect people with a more educated background to work for that money? The market will just dry up. We can barely get people now, especially people to work with these very disabled students and deal with their physical and mental needs all day. (03-432-21)

A director of special education confirmed this observation:

The sad truth is that it is very hard to find skillful paraprofessionals who are willing to accept the low pay we can offer. You can make more money at a fast food restaurant with a lot less stress. So we hire the best that we can find and then hope they can handle the work. I have no idea who we are going to get following the new guidelines. (11-03-51)

In this complex tension of mandated special needs and state requirements to meet prescribed and regulated curriculum standards, classroom teachers face the reality of students who do not test well, require additional scarce time, and ultimately, bring down the class (and school) averages. Limited local school budgets strain to provide the additional supports and resources these students need.

I teach high school science and I think we lead the country in identification of special needs. We can have 20% of a class on IEPs [individual education plans] on my level. Accommodating those requirements is just added in on top of everything else we are doing. You know scheduling alone becomes a nightmare. When 20% of your class in on IEPs and then you have them moving in and out of your classroom for special help and then you test them on information they maybe never got or didn't get in the way the state tests, they're going to fail and that score is reflected in your grade-level averages. These students have to have special education services but they also have to get the regular classroom instruction. It is an impossible situation. (01-2-87)

A special education teacher also saw the effects of these pressures:

I think special education students will continue to be a scapegoat. Right now, these kids are already targeted by the state tests as dragging down the scores. We started looking at the yearly reading test a year ago. I think most people assumed that it was our special education kids who are dragging down the scores. It turns out that in a lot of cases, they aren't but that was the assumption. The state results showed that our kids couldn't read the questions. They maybe knew the answers but couldn't handle the format. But I'll be honest about this. The typical developmentally delayed child doesn't have a prayer of scoring anything beyond basic on the state test. That child will drag down our averages. (03-42-27)

As teachers consider the problems of painfully limited district budgets and which students will receive the time, attention, and resources that are available, they are locked in serious debates that challenge ethical foundations:

> I think it is a huge problem. Balancing the needs of all children and being able to be honest about it—that is a tough issue to talk about. You don't want to look at a child who has so many things against him/her and say, "I don't want to work with this child" or "I don't want to spend money for the services for this child." The problem is that you have a pot that is this big filled with time and attention and money. And how to be fair about where it goes . . . I think that's a big issue. Something has to give, and I see it happening now with us. I see it happening with me. There is not enough time in the school day to support the concept of inclusion. We say we are inclusionary and every child will be in a regular classroom and I agree that is the right idea. But there is not enough support to make it work. The kids suffer for it. I don't think most people realize that. (03-3-60)

> We have to get more support from the state. Right now the state will not add funding. It just says the schools aren't doing their job, which really fuels the adversarial role between parents of special-needs kids and the school. The federal government comes up with all of these rules and then gives us about 12% of what the rules are costing us. It just builds resentments. When you have a child who is costing the district $50,000 everybody knows who that child is. People feel the costs of that child's education are depriving other students of district funds. It creates an atmosphere that isn't good for anyone. (07-43-25)

> There is already so much resentment financially about what special education kids cost the district as well as the time they require from the teacher. If the special education kids also score poorly on the test and the school is one of the schools that needs improvement, then the resentment can only grow. (05-17-23)

While frustration over limited time for instruction and the pressures of regulated testing is expressed throughout this study, its effects are most chilling when applied to special-needs students. Requiring additional planning, reteaching, and the threat of legal recourse, these students are a focus of growing resentment.

I find myself frustrated with the ones who just can't get it fast enough. Oh, my gosh, it is like the Kentucky Derby with the small kids. I've got a couple of them, we have to go slow, take time, and they still don't get it. And then these tests come and they say not just how these kids are doing but what kind of teacher I am. You know? What do I do? And what does that say to parents? And then the district office comes at us all because of these poor kids who just can't learn that fast. (09-2-14)

I don't like saying this, but they are making us very resentful of the added burden of special-needs kids. With no support or time to help these kids, I only want to have the kids that have half a chance of passing these tests. (10-1-90)

It makes you not want them in your class. Let's face it. If your test scores are going to be publicized for you as a teacher or other teachers are going to see it or other administrators, you don't want those kids in your class because they are just going to bring you down. It does not lend itself to wanting to work with these kids. (12-04-33)

A teacher concluded:

It's easy to solve this problem. You don't want kids with special needs in your classroom. They slow things down. They require too much extra time and we just don't have it anymore. (09-2-18)

TEACHERS, STUDENTS, AND NCLB

We know that the relationship between teachers and their students is critical in the learning process. We know that students learn best when they feel their teachers like them and take a personal interest in them. Similarly, we know that teachers feel greater job satisfaction when they have a personal connection with their students and can guide them through development in all domains. This interactive relationship is mutually beneficial and rewarding.

This relationship takes on different tones as teachers describe adaptations in their teaching to conform to standardized teaching practices. They use phrases like "mutants" and "robots" to describe how standardized approaches to teaching impersonalize their work. They express worry that district standards are actually limiting their own efforts to consider all domains of the developing child into their instructional design. Additionally, they describe the emotional needs of many students needing very specific interpersonal connections between the teacher and student in order for learning to occur. Teachers see their opportunities to develop these relationships increasingly diminished as their teaching time becomes more structured and regulated.

The teachers' views of students are altered with reform pressures. Consistent with national findings, teachers describe a growing frustration and, in some cases, intolerance with students who are not motivated to learn or are not able to keep up with other students. They describe these students as requiring extra time and attention teachers do not have. Students who don't understand material in the time teachers have to present it are a problem for teachers who feel compelled to keep the rest of the class moving forward. These students' poor achievement is seen as a detriment to class averages. Their academic problems and their effects on test results compound through the grade levels.

Special-needs populations are a serious concern as well for teachers in this study. Teachers are responsible for providing the mandated support these students require. They often see these students as not getting the additional professional support they need. While some teachers describe this work as meaningful, they also see it as very time consuming. They see regular students "paying the price" for special-needs instruction and support as teacher time is diverted from regular instruction to attending to the most needy students. For special-needs students, these interpretations are very serious. Their presence becomes a liability for teachers who recognize the impact of these students on the nonmandated students' opportunity to learn. They see class averages on standardized testing impacted and they see their own accountability jeopardized.

Teachers and administrators agree that there are no easy answers to this dilemma. While all participants in this study feel that there are clear benefits with standardized guidelines, there remains the reality that there just isn't enough time or adequate resources in most schools to do what is required to ensure success for all students. The struggles are compounded as NCLB applies sanctions and financial consequences to low-scoring schools that serve high proportions of at-risk populations. Students already identified as "at risk" or "high need" face the double jeopardy of also being an expensive risk to their schools and districts. These troubling budgetary facts and punitive accountability measures seriously impact the relationship we recognize and value between teachers and their students.

6

Defining, Training, and Keeping
High-Quality Teachers

We will work to ensure that all of our nation's schools have the high-quality teachers they need to boost student achievement, both by recruiting new, highly qualified teachers and by providing current teachers access to rigorous professional development.

—President George W. Bush
(U.S. Department of Education, 2002, p. 40)

No Child Left Behind (NCLB) is grounded in the understanding that teachers are the reason schools succeed or fail. The federal call for "high-quality" teachers is the built-in guarantee that our education system can meet the goal of every child succeeding if standards for teaching training are raised and classroom expectations for teachers are clearly defined. To underscore the importance placed on this federal guideline, the act ensures compliance by requiring states to meet federal definitions of "highly qualified" in order to remain eligible for federal funding. While analyzing the reasons for school failure remains open to serious investigation, the desire to have competent teachers in every classroom is shared by all who are invested in the debate. Exactly what constitutes a "qualified teacher" and how to measure those qualifiers remain hotly contested issues.

Federal guidelines require teachers to be certified or licensed in the state in which they are teaching. Teachers are required to be proficient in their subject matter. Proficiency can be demonstrated by majoring in the subject in college, passing a subject-knowledge test, or obtaining advanced certification in the subject. Teachers who were in the classroom when the law took effect are considered "proficient" if they meet those same qualifiers or if they meet separate qualifiers set by individual states, known as a High Objective Uniform State Standard of Evaluation, or HOUSSE. These requirements were originally established to be met by the end of the 2006 school year. In the fall of 2005, Secretary of Education Margaret Spellings extended the deadline to spring of 2007 if states could prove that they have made sufficient progress in meeting this requirement to earn a reprieve.

HISTORIC BENCHMARKS OF TEACHER QUALITY

Expectations for teachers have historically reflected the political climate at any given time. As trends and issues change, curriculum and classroom expectations shift. In comparison, colleges and universities have enjoyed considerable latitude in defining programs to train teachers entering the profession. State boards of education have assumed varying levels of authority by establishing guidelines and monitoring their school districts. Local school districts have had the authority to define their own teacher expectations and supervise teacher performances through their school administrators and local school board leadership. National and state teacher unions joined the conversation over the years with significant "bread and butter" contract issues concerning tenure, wages, and benefits, while providing professional resources and legal supports to members.

It is not surprising that the reform agenda sent shock waves through the teaching profession with its fundamental focus on the supervision and systematic evaluation of classroom teachers. The intensity and focus of these guidelines mark the first time in the history of public education that the federal government has taken the initiative to define teacher quality and to include fiscally punitive measures for noncompliance. While academic standards and assessment practices have always defined achievement for students, it is the new link between uniform teacher competency standards and student test scores that is the driving force behind the changes and the ultimate determiner of reform success.

DEFINING TEACHER QUALITY

The federal government has broadened its net in pursuing quality teachers by involving colleges and universities in its action plan. The Washington-based National Council for Accreditation of Teacher Education (NCATE) established standards in 2001 requiring teacher training programs to provide evidence that they have designed and are implementing monitoring systems throughout the teacher training experience. Measurements include documenting pedagogical instruction and skills and tracking opportunities for actual classroom teaching experiences before graduation. States are also required to report the percentage of graduating students who pass the licensing exams. The fact that each state is allowed to set its own passing scores complicates comparisons between states. Teacher training programs are required to use their data to evaluate their own programs and implement improvements based on findings. NCATE has accredited about half of the nation's 1,200 schools of education. There has also been movement to increase monitoring efforts on the state level. Fourteen states now require education programs to monitor the success of graduates in the classroom (Honawar, 2007). On-the-job evaluations determine the next steps, including instructional intervention and additional classroom training.

The indisputable fact that the teacher-student relationship is at its core relational makes quantifying teacher quality complicated and difficult. Researchers from the business community and education scholars have worked independently as well as in partnership with colleges and universities to provide data and structure in these efforts. While providing a limited scope, the input-output model associated with industry has provided some guidelines for the federal reform plan.

Teacher "input" models include those characteristics that a teacher brings to the classroom. Examples would be teacher training and certification requirements. Test scores of prospective teachers on college entrance exams as well as basic skills tests are used as possible predictors of ultimate student success (Ferguson, 1998; Ferguson & Ladd, 1996). Advanced degrees also seem to impact student success. Deep-content knowledge, especially in science and math, has been shown to have a positive impact on student achievement (Monk, 1994). Years of experience in teaching also correlate with student success up to the fifth year of teaching, when benefits seem to level off. These factors in combination provide some insight into measurable factors that preclude instruction.

Under NCLB guidelines, teacher "outputs" are student test scores and are the primary indicators of teaching quality. The precarious nature of test scores in schools has already been discussed. Factors such as school leadership, changing curriculum, and shifting student populations impact classroom stability and instructional opportunity. We know that student performance on any given day is impacted by home stability, absenteeism, general health, and the relational climate in the classroom. In combination, these external and internal variables seriously compromise the reliability of an output model based on a single test score.

An alternative approach that is gaining increasing approval is the use of "value-added" assessments. While these tests are also administered on a yearly basis, the actual scores track gains students are predicted to make based on past performance. One example comes from a study on value-added assessments in Tennessee. Students taught for three consecutive years by teachers identified as "high-quality teachers" made gains of approximately 50 percentile points on standardized tests over students who did not have those benefits (Sanders & Rivers, 1996). The benefit of this model is that students are measured against their own progress rather than being compared to preestablished grade level standards.

Even with these concrete and measurable criteria, defining teacher quality remains elusive. State legislators and teacher preparation programs continue working on measurable criteria. Quantitative studies bring in data each year to be analyzed and evaluated. The simple fact that teaching and learning are dependent upon relationships and the unpredictability of human development remain sticking points in these efforts.

TEACHER CERTIFICATION: THE STATE TEACHER ASSESSMENT

Implementation of NCLB guidelines requires new teachers to pass a basic competency test in order to be certified. This includes passing a content area test in one of four subjects: math, English language arts, general science, or social studies. These standards are supported by NCATE, the National Board for Professional Teaching Standards (NBPTS), and Goal

4 of the Goals 2000 plan, which addresses teacher education and professional development (U.S. Department of Education, 1994). The federal measurement of teacher quality is also viewed as an ongoing process. In addition to initial certification or licensing requirements, NCLB requires states to define some means of ensuring ongoing "rigorous professional development" for practicing teachers. Federal guidelines require school districts to focus on research-based instructional strategies that are aligned with state content standards and implementation plans that provide adequate time for training to be effective (U.S. Department of Education, 2002).

Teachers in this study supported the concept of professional standards. They also supported the identification and removal of unqualified people from teaching:

> Most teachers want standards and want their colleagues to be at that level. There are very few teachers out there who will honestly say "It's okay that Mrs. Jones isn't a good teacher, but it's all right, she's been here for 30 years." I don't think any of us feel that way. We know that this is a year in a child's life and only the best and the brightest and the most capable should have the responsibility to bring that child through the year. (03-3-39)

National teacher unions also support standards for teachers. A state-level union official described not wanting the government making these decisions:

> I think it's right. In the past a teacher could be completely unqualified and still get a job. We have to protect the integrity of the profession. If we don't, some bozo in the legislature will. (07-1-16)

Teachers agree that the "integrity of the profession" needs protecting. No teachers feel incompetent teachers should be allowed to continue teaching. Teachers also recognize the difficulty of quantifying the complex nature of their work. A focus on content skills is seen as having limited value when attempting to identify competent teaching:

> I think we have to have a way to remove teachers who aren't doing their jobs. Other than that, I don't think the other teacher competency thing is really necessary. I see teachers who just shouldn't be teaching. And I don't think

that has anything to do with how competent they are in math, or English, or how intelligent they are. I don't think you can pick that out on those kinds of tests. Maybe you need tests to use as a piece for getting these people out of teaching. You'll catch a few that way. I've heard of a few examples. But that is pretty rare. It's more an attitude about teaching and kids and dedication that really mark a good teacher from one who doesn't care. (11-1-28)

Qualities of "attitude about teaching" and "dedication" are seen as authentic indicators of a "good teacher" by this teacher. Another teacher supports and broadens the concept of qualities of teacher competency to include professional expertise, a repertoire of teaching strategies, and skillful interpretation of how kids learn:

So much of teaching is management. We have to know how to pull all sorts of resources together quickly, have a solid repertoire of teaching techniques, and know when to use which ones—a range of techniques for handling different kinds of kids with different kinds of problems, setting up an environment that is interesting, constant monitoring of how different kids are handling a lesson, a unit, program. It's not just passing on information. I wish it was that simple. Anybody who can read can pass on information. (09-3-35)

Teachers acknowledge that content tests do not assess classroom management skills, interpersonal skills, or the ability to apply pedagogical skills. Instead, the current testing tools assess competence in basic skills and, in some cases, whether an individual does or does not have enough knowledge of content to be minimally successful in the classroom. They argue that a test of knowledge is not a measure of teaching competence. Rather, it can identify what is missing in specific areas of content knowledge. Content testing is seen as "catching a few" unqualified teaching candidates. Teachers and research conclude that state competency tests do not address the complexity of skillful teaching.

In a conversation with a member of the New Hampshire State Board of Teaching Standards, I presented some of the local teachers' concerns about providing a more complete competency measurement that would include elements of pedagogy. She explained how "issues of cost" limited the state from addressing broader interpretations of teaching:

Well, pedagogical skills separate teachers from people who just know a lot about a topic. That is what makes teaching a profession. We know it's im-

portant to consider that, but it's an issue of cost. The competency tests ensure content standards and that's part of the picture for good teaching. Those
skills are very expensive to test. Adding on pedagogical skills would be a
huge cost that the state just can't take on. People don't understand that about
teaching. (06-TR-AR-2-53)

In most states, teacher assessment priorities remain fixed with curriculum standards and reflect a very limited definition of teacher competency.
The state assessment has no authenticity in identifying those qualities that
teachers feel separate them from "people who just know a lot about a
topic." Additional costs do not justify the results. In contrast, teachers feel
that the "results" are the reason standards are needed. Policy makers turn
to standardized testing to define teacher competency because it is easier
to judge people numerically rather than qualitatively.

Teachers in this study support reform standards that regulate new teachers entering the profession. They also acknowledge the limited value of
content-based competency tests as a method to "weed out" some undesirable candidates. Teachers disagree with the focus of the current state assessment model used in most states because it does not recognize the complexity of teaching and does not screen candidates for those competencies.
Teachers argue that state competency tests do not identify teacher candidates who are prepared to meet the challenges of the classroom.

PROFESSIONAL DEVELOPMENT

The federal measurement of teacher quality is also viewed as an ongoing
process. In addition to initial certification or licensing requirements,
NCLB requires states to define some means of ensuring "on-going, rigorous professional development" for practicing teachers. Federal guidelines
require school districts to focus on research-based instructional strategies
that are aligned with state content standards and implementation plans that
provide adequate time for training to be effective. It is estimated that districts spend 2% to 5% of their annual budgets on professional development each year (Noyce, 2006).

Written standards for professional development have increased in recent years. Providing funding and time for these opportunities have also
increased. In these efforts, state initiatives define what constitutes teacher

development opportunities and what professional opportunities qualify for ongoing teacher recertification. These professional development opportunities align directly with state improvement initiatives of standardized curriculum and state assessment. They provide definitions of effective teaching and what choices teachers have to improve their work. The goal in these efforts is quantifiable. Teacher development opportunities are designed to produce improved student test scores.

Classroom teachers in this study support state efforts to provide professional development opportunities that enhance their work. Teachers do not agree with the restrictions on their professional growth choices. One teacher saw this regulation as resulting in a "sort of compromise" between what teachers in her district wanted and the goals established by district administrators:

> Now we have staff development committees for teachers and the districts have certain goals that they'd like to have as district goals. We look for professional development that goes along with that. A lot of times, it is administrative decisions and those tend to be not as successful as the ones teachers suggest. But we do have input, it's sort of a compromise. (03-4-58)

Another teacher discussed problems with standardized approaches to teacher development and how state designed workshops didn't necessarily relate to pertinent issues for teachers:

> I think one of the things teachers say when they come back from professional workshops is "Yes, I think it was good, but . . . [laughter]. I could have used those six hours better with my colleagues. You can always learn from outside workshops, but you need information that is relevant to your school. Too many times, the information is based on a general theme that could be summarized in much less time if they would just check with us first to see what we need. (03-1-32, 33)

Teachers raised concerns about the limitations district-defined professional development opportunities had in meeting their own definitions of professional needs. They felt pedagogical theory and applications as well as the interpersonal skills of effective teaching were missing from the new state descriptions of teacher development guidelines:

We're dealing with human beings. You can have a wonderful knowledge base, but if you don't understand how children learn and how they grow intellectually, and socially, and physically, and how they interact with others, and at different ages, I don't see how you can teach. (09-3-33)

TEACHER QUALITY AND SCHOOL IMPROVEMENT

Definitions of "standards" in teaching, learning, and assessment have been fundamental control mechanisms in the current reform design. Researcher Darling-Hammond (1990) explains presumptions about these definitions:

> Reform design presumes that schools can be made to improve [only] if standards are set and incentives established that force school people to pay attention to them. Essentially this line of thinking assumes that problems exist either because educators don't have precise enough targets to aim for, because they aren't trying hard enough, or both. Supplying concrete goals and using both carrots and stick to move educators to pursue them are the presumed answers to under performance. (p. 287)

Educational researchers Giroux (1988) and Osterman and Kottkamp (1993) argue against definitions of professionalism that are limited to successful implementation of standardized curriculum. They suggest that professionalism should reflect the complexity of the classroom and the skills needed to address it. Cogan (1953) describes teachers as requiring specialized knowledge and commitment to continuing inquiry to advance knowledge that may be relevant to the classroom. Moore (1970) describes conditions of practice that allowed teachers to apply this knowledge freely to the practical affairs of the classroom setting and to use their knowledge, judgment, and skill within the structures of the ethical code of the profession. Case (1986) feels that essential characteristics defining a modern profession include knowledge, commitment to inquiry, service to a public good, and a professional network. Researchers assert that current definitions of quality and professional teaching standards do not support principles of professionalism that are fundamental to effective teaching and learning.

A final consideration in teacher standards is the underlying assumption that the quality of America's teachers has been in a steady decline. Commission reports predicted that national teaching standards would reverse this trend (Carnegie Forum, 1986; Holmes Group, 1986; National Governors' Association, 1986). The National Education Association reported in 1992 that the proportion of teachers holding advanced degree qualifications had actually been climbing for the previous three decades. In 1965, about 15% of the teaching force held less than a four-year degree. By 1991, this figure had dropped to 0.6%. During the past 30 years, the percentage of teachers holding a master's or doctorate degree increased dramatically and at the end of the 1990's hovered at about 50%. Berliner and Biddle (1995) argue that teachers, as a group, have impressive academic credentials. They conclude, "Given that teachers represent by far the largest profession in the nation, this is a remarkable record" (p. 339).

STATE REFORM AND TEACHER COMPETENCY: IF YOU DON'T CUT THE MUSTARD, YOU'RE OUT . . .

The third feature of state reform efforts is a call for state governments to define their own standards for teacher competency. "Poor teaching" in this framework is seen as responsible for "poor test scores." Some states demand all teachers—even those with years of teaching experience—to pass a state competency test. The public has also historically wanted measurable proof that teachers are qualified to instruct. In the 1988 *Gallup Poll of the Public's Attitudes Towards Public Schools*, 86% of the respondents indicated that experienced teachers periodically should be required to pass a competency examination in their teaching area (Gallup & Elam, 1988).

A New Hampshire classroom teacher who is a state leader in reform described the intentions of their bill as a negative state action against teachers:

> There was a wish on the part of legislators to have teacher training as a way to get rid of teachers and not support them in their learning, but not to say, "You don't cut the mustard so you're out." This attitude was perceived to be more promoting negativity toward teachers as opposed to really having a function of getting rid of bad teachers. Everybody has been in agreement that you have to get rid of poor teachers but you have to give

them a chance to make the kinds of specific improvement that are needed
and if they can't do that, well, then, true, you help them out and you get
them out of the profession. But that was not the intent of what the legislature was about. (03-3-52)

A lobbyist for the state teachers' union explained the union's argument
with the initiative:

> The concept of a test to enter the profession is one thing. The problem we
> had was the periodic testing. You don't periodically test lawyers. (03-7-25)

The governor of the state vetoed their bill, but did set up a commission to
study testing of new teachers. A union leader who was a member of that
commission interpreted their work as an effort to gain some control in
teaching standards:

> Originally, the intent of the bill was to establish a way to get rid of unwanted
> teachers quicker. The union went to the governor and protested so she
> formed our commission to look at performance reviews in lieu of legislated
> authority. The result was a plan to examine staff performance reviews on the
> local level. We also examined criteria for recertification that included input
> from union representatives and the State Department Professional Board.
> That is also in place, now. We saw a need to get control of criteria for teach-
> ing standards before a bunch of politicians who don't know anything about
> education started setting up with the rules. (06-1-4, 7)

The commission identified three measurements of teacher competency.
First, they defined initial state teacher certification criteria. New definitions of teacher qualifications included state-authorized competency tests.
Second, professional development regulations were established that redefined state recertification requirements for practicing teachers. Third,
teacher performance evaluations in their schools took on the added criteria of student test scores. High student test scores indicated teacher competency. Low test scores indicated the need for state-defined teacher development to improve competency. In combination, the commission
presented a comprehensive definition of teacher competency. Each definition directly reflected adoption of state curriculum frameworks and state
assessment goals into new standards for teachers.

STATE RECERTIFICATION REQUIREMENTS:
MANY OF OUR CURRENT TEACHERS ARE UNPREPARED

State policy makers also determined that new competencies were required for ongoing teacher development and recertification. They looked to NCATE, NBPTS, and Goals 2000 for guidelines in this process. The National Goals 2000 Resource Panel (1996) provided recommendations on teacher development with a new focus on national goals for the improvement of instruction:

> While there are many ingredients for successful school reform, it all comes down to the classroom teacher. Indeed, the success of the entire school reform movement is dependent upon teachers acquiring the skills, perspectives and knowledge necessary to transform the learning of all students. However, because we only now fully appreciate the ways of teaching complex subject matter to diverse students, many of our current teachers remain under- or unprepared. Insufficient or inadequate pre-service and inappropriate or incoherent in-service teacher education retard the effort to realize the national education goals. (p. 1)

This introduction identified classroom teachers as the key implementers of reform objectives. The premise that all students were in need of being "transformed" in learning was coupled with the need for retraining of teachers who were not adequately prepared to teach to the federal objectives. This process was seen as "retarded" by insufficient or incoherent in-service. The panel suggested that control of teachers' in-servicing opportunities would result in meeting the identified academic needs of students. Professional development opportunities that focused on national curriculum guidelines would ensure a teaching community that would be prepared to meet the federal education goals.

State legislatures adopted these recommendations in the form of statewide education improvement and assessment bills. The bills established alignment between state student assessment scores and decisions about school programs that would include focused in-service education programs for teachers. They authorized the state departments of education to use the state student assessment tool not only as an indicator of student achievement, but also as an indicator of school and district success. This effort merged the previously separate functions of student assessment and teacher professional development. State standards outlined what teachers should know and be able to do toward incorporation of the state curriculum frameworks into their instruction. Professional development opportunities were identified as the means to help teachers do this.

State definitions of teacher competency focus on the instructional practice of the classroom teachers. Teacher competency is based on how effectively they incorporate curriculum frameworks into their teaching. Accountability is defined in terms of student test scores. To ensure focus on these goals, teacher development opportunities are recommended that support curriculum guidelines and assist teachers in monitoring and adjusting instructional decisions following student testing.

While teachers agree that technical training is important in reaching specific curriculum goals, they remain passionate about the emotional and social needs of children. Teachers discussed the real need for professional development that helps teachers to reach students with increasingly complex learning and behavior challenges. They felt professional development in these areas superseded focus on test scores.

Oh, I think help with understanding these troubled kids is very important. How well they do has a lot to do with their perception of their relationship with me. If they aren't comfortable with me, they have across-the-board anxiety that affects how well they do. If our relationship is comfortable and they can trust me and I know that I am there to help them with rules that are reasonable and we are working together, things are going to work out fine. Then they'll be able to do their work to the best of their ability. (11-1-2)

Another teacher spoke about the challenges that children bring to school, and the skills teachers needed to deal with them:

We have lots and lots of kids who come to school with too much emotional baggage and they come with academic needs that students didn't have before. We have to deal with the emotional baggage because if we don't, they can't function in school and if they can't function, it will affect everyone else's ability to learn. They react by being disruptive. Other times they will just withdraw. That won't affect the other kids, but it will affect the child and me. I can't emotionally handle knowing that a child isn't learning. I mean I have to find a way to help that child. (11-1-6)

Teachers also talked about the diverse academic challenges in a classroom and how they must be skilled to address these differences:

> In fourth grade, we get kids who abilities range from first grade to fourth.
> Then we get kids with special needs whose emotional needs are all over the
> board. I have to adjust my instruction for all of those kids, while staying fo-
> cused on content goals. I am continually readjusting my strategies to meet
> all of those needs while trying to give them what they need individually. It
> is very challenging but I think I make a difference in their lives. (02-2-13)

Teachers' perceptions of competency rested not only in content knowledge, but also in the highly developed pedagogical theory that addressed
diverse learning styles, wide ranges in student skills, and the social needs
of children in the classroom. Teachers saw the federal interpretation of
teaching as "an exchange of content knowledge between teachers and
their students" as a limited interpretation of the work they do. Additionally, this interpretation did not support their intellectual growth. Theorist
Schaefer (1967) describes the need of "scholarship" for teachers 40 years
ago. His conclusions remain pertinent today:

> When divorced from appropriate scholarship in substance and pedagogy,
> teaching resembles employment as an educational sales clerk. Almost
> everyone concedes that teaching is or should be an intellectual calling, an
> occupation emphasizing the transmission of intellectual goods and the use
> of intelligence in making instructional decisions. But an ever-sharper divi-
> sion of function—between those who contribute to the production of knowl-
> edge or its synthesis for pedagogical purposes and those who routinely dis-
> tribute it in packaged form in schools—deprives the teacher of his inherent
> intellectual rights. By concentrating on the distributive function alone, the
> school effectively imprisons rather than liberates the full power of the
> teacher's mind. (p. 2)

Cohn and Kottkamp (1993) conclude current reform intentions are not
attainable *without* pedagogical consideration. They found that the
achievement of teacher instructional purposes was highly dependent on
pedagogical understandings and interpersonal skills:

> What most educational reform proposals fail to acknowledge, let alone ad-
> dress is the relationship between interpersonal and pedagogical processes and
> instructional outcomes. Instead, they consistently focus almost exclusively on

academic or cognitive outcomes with little or no attention to the means required to reach those ends, particularly in the changing context of schooling.
What teachers know, however, is that without establishing a positive learning
climate and finding pedagogical strategies to interest students in content, the
desired academic outcomes will continue to elude them. (p. 48)

The National Goals 2000 Resource Panel official rhetoric also confirmed the need for teacher skills beyond the transmission of content:

> The interactions that occur between student and teacher, the opportunities
> for students to construct knowledge, the modeling of appropriate behavior
> by teachers, the setting of high rigorous expectations, the existence of sup-
> portive classroom environments, the use of results-driven practices and per-
> formance-based assessments, are dependent upon skilled, knowledgeable,
> and compassionate teachers. The role of the teacher is central. (U.S. De-
> partment of Education, 1994, p. 3)

District plans for teachers in this study did not include considerations
of "skilled, knowledgeable, and compassionate teachers." These district
plans were designed to require teachers to focus exclusively on teaching
methods and interpretations that supported state curriculum guidelines.
Teacher competency was defined in measurable outcomes of student content testing. Recertification requirements restricted professional growth
options to alignment with state reform objectives. These changes promoted conformity and control over definitions of a "good" teacher, and
what skills a teacher needed to remain certified.

TEACHERS' UNIONS AND COMPETENCY

I spoke at length with union leaders in New Hampshire and Minnesota on
how they were responding to the state-controlled decisions on teacher development. One representative saw the competency standards as basically
a financial burden on teachers. He also projected further restrictions for
teachers:

> I think the future will bring further restrictions on how teachers meet recer-
> tification requirements. We have to be in there to make sure it's fair and op-
> portunities to do that are spelled out in the contract negotiations. Districts

don't like that. In the business community, the company pays for all training plus it reimburses the person for their time. In the schools, teachers are
lucky if they get tuition reimbursement. If the government is going to require training, it should also reimburse the costs. We are working to get that
into contracts. (07-1-9, 11)

Union representatives saw their role as working for teacher reimbursement for state-required in-servicing. The issues of control over teachers'
authority to define standards in their profession or choose their own professional development options were not recognized.

As definitions of teacher competency become state mandated and increasingly controlled, attention to content proficiency of teachers and students gains importance and government sanction. Student test scores become the driving force in the measurement of competency and criteria for
professional development for teachers. The role of the teacher as a spe-
cialist in pedagogical theory is minimized, professional development is
limited to standardized curricular interpretation, and the work of teachers
is reduced to producing high test scores. Teachers in this study argued that
focusing only on content understanding diminished the true nature of
teaching and suggested simplified and inaccurate public perceptions of
their actual work. They asserted that their perspectives and participation
were required for an accurate definition of professional competency:

I think teachers have to be included in deciding competency. Teaching is such
a unique profession. I don't think people outside of the profession can truly
understand what it means to be a teacher. Only those who do it can really appreciate what the job entails and what you need to do to be a good teacher. It
needs to come from the profession of educators, from people who are in the
classroom every day and understand what we are facing. (W17-12-35)

DEFINING TEACHER QUALITY

Defining teacher quality is a fundamental requirement in the federal education reform package. The outcome of the yearly state assessments is the
key indicator of success or failure and it has several functions. First, it is
the primary means to determine standards of achievement for students.
Second, it has evolved into a driving force behind teachers' efforts to in-

corporate matching curriculum areas into their teaching objectives. Third, it is the primary tool to measure teacher competency. And fourth, it is the criteria to determine appropriate teacher development opportunities in districts and recertification requirements within the states. Teachers approach the yearly tests with understandable trepidation.

Teacher training institutions, researchers, teachers' unions, and members of the business community have also added their ideas about teacher quality as state legislators and district leaders have formulated state plans. As definitions and control shifted from local districts to state and federal interpretations of change, teachers have responded to new definitions of their purpose, their competence, and their authority in state reform conversations. New regulations on the work of teachers have resulted in fundamental changes. Understandings about curriculum, assessment procedures, and appropriate teaching methodology are redefined to embrace standardized procedures. Powerful regulators and compliance strategies are included in the reform design to ensure district adoption of state and federal objectives and teacher conformity.

Teachers want to see improvements in their profession. They want to see new graduates join the profession thoroughly prepared to meet the demands of the classroom. Teachers also shared clear directives on what they feel is needed for authentic professional development and pedagogical support. They need time to plan and to collaborate with other teachers. They want diagnostic and prescriptive support from district specialists to design and meet consistent and attainable standards for their students. They need high-quality professional development programs that address the real issues in the classroom and they need curriculum resources that address and support the complex needs of diverse students. They want training to strengthen their own instructional and assessment strategies and they want administrators who can provide the leadership needed to bring about real school improvement. They also ask for serious attention to the neglected environments in which many teachers and their students work.

7

The Wall of Silence

Teachers argue that they know more about the real problems in education and the real changes that need to be made than the authorities who have taken control over education policy. They do not express these observations and conclusions to education authorities and decision makers. One teacher described this paradox:

> I look at us as a profession and I think, we know better than anybody what's going on with this profession and we know who is doing a good job and who is not doing a good job and who has the skills and who drags things down and all that. But somewhere in here, I don't see us talking about it. I don't see us expressing this. There's this wall of silence. And these raging voices from the outside telling us what's wrong and what's not wrong . . . and we are silent. (09-3-99)

Researchers have identified classroom teachers as having the least level of authority in the reform hierarchy (Apple, 1990; Fuhrman & Elmore, 1994; Gilles, Geletta, & Daniels, 1994; Murphy, 1990). Cohn and Kottkamp (1993) described their view of the classroom teachers' place in reform definition:

> Teachers live at the center of the maelstrom of rhetoric, vilification, and conflict over making our educational system better. They have been expected to "shape up" and implement the reforms that others have developed. They have been treated more like uninformed hired hands than

professionals to whom we entrust our most precious asset. They have
been the last to be consulted when we consider what is broken and how
to fix it. Their voices have not and still do not inform the actions taken to
rectify what reformers believe to be the matter with education in the
United States. (p. xv)

As implementers of reform, teachers spoke candidly about the effects
of reform in their classrooms and in their districts. They described
grave concerns about changes they were incorporating as having serious consequences for students as well as themselves. Additionally,
teachers knew exactly which reform definitions were bringing positive
change and which policies were actually counterproductive to state reform objectives of improved instruction and learning. In my interviews
with teachers, I asked them to explain their sense of authority to address these issues. They described how their relationships with school
administration, the state departments of education, and the teachers'
unions defined and controlled their power to question or challenge reform policy.

Loveless (1994) argues that excluding classroom teachers from these
critical conversations has resulted in a reform package that does not address the complexities of the tasks of classroom teachers and cannot
achieve its purposes:

It is not the conservative complaint that national standards usurp local authority over education that tarnishes the latest effort. Nor is it the liberal
complaint that standards supply new justifications for condemning the historically disadvantaged members of our society. Both are legitimate concerns. But unfortunately, in accommodating these and other concerns, Goals
2000 lost its focus. What we have now looks more like 2000 educational
goals—and a missed opportunity to sharpen the purpose of schooling in
America. Moreover, the failure of the standards to speak directly to teachers and students renders the recent debate largely irrelevant to the nation's
classrooms. (p. 52)

Scholars conclude that excluding teachers from reform conversations in
meaningful ways has resulted in reform objectives that do not address the
reality of the classroom setting and compromise reform success (Apple,
1990; Chubb, 1988; Cohn & Kottkamp, 1993).

TEACHERS' FEEDBACK ON ASSESSMENTS: THEY DON'T REALLY WANT TO HEAR IT

Classroom teachers in this study talked about their frustrations with standardized restrictions and interpretations on their teaching. They also described efforts to express these frustrations to state officials. In some states, teachers were asked to participate in early policy decisions. An example of this occurred in New Hampshire. In 1997, teachers were invited to meet and discuss reform objectives with representatives from the State Department of Education. A teacher in this study recalled one of these meetings as a time not for discussion, but for passive listening:

> We were all called together to meet with Mr. ___ to talk about reform. Some teachers tried to talk about what wasn't working, but, you know, they don't really want to hear that stuff. The principal and Mr. ___ were very clear about how the standards are in place. They really just wanted to tell us what to do, so we just ended up listening to what they had to say. (10-1-23)

Additionally, some teachers talked about writing letters to state department heads describing their concerns about testing and its impact on their students and their schools:

> The first year we tried to get their attention. We sat down with the whole grade level and wrote a five-page letter. Nothing came back! I know teachers in other schools did this, too. They were getting complaints, but no one was listening. (10-1-53)

The following year the State Department of Education created review committees for teachers. A spokesperson for the State Department of Education described these committee meetings as an opportunity to get feedback from teachers about reform in their districts:

> Yes, well, you know, we want teachers to feel like they are a part of all of this, so the department organized the review committees so teachers could talk about what was actually happening in their districts. This really helped, because people who wanted to get more involved could volunteer. The committees have really helped with that. (06-2-1)

A classroom teacher in this study volunteered to be on a curriculum review committee. She described the first two meetings as State Department of Education efforts to promote compliance with the state reform agendas:

> I think they are trying to respond to teachers. I am on this committee that is set up to gather information. There have been so many complaints. These are teachers on all levels. There are administrators, too, who are just fed up. At the first meeting, we read reports from other countries, comparing the U.S. scores to theirs. At the next meeting, we were supposed to bring examples of how our districts were implementing the frameworks. Now we are giving out surveys to our teachers to see how they are improving in their teaching. I will bring those surveys to the next meeting and we are supposed to study them. (10-2-55)

Teachers understood the purpose of these committees was to provide an opportunity for "teachers to respond" to the state tests. In reality, the goal of the committee shifted to analysis of how districts and teachers were implementing reform in their classrooms. I asked the teacher on the curriculum review committee about this shift in purpose and if she ever had a chance to express the concerns she had about reform standards:

> No, you can't tell them a thing. At first we tried to talk about concerns, but now, Mr. ___, the head of the committee, is becoming very defensive. At the last meeting he told us the frameworks are in place and you will work with them. So basically, he meant they are there, and we have to figure out how to make them work . . . don't complain because it's not going to change. He was very defensive. Originally, he was very open, but by the second meeting, he was very short and didn't want to hear what we were saying. (10-2-55)

The classroom teachers on the review committee understood that their original function was to gather and present district response to the state curriculum frameworks and state assessment. Once there, the work of the committee was reinvented to actually describe their own district progress and report on teachers' progress toward improvement of adoption of state goals. Teachers who did try to speak about teachers' concerns were censored. They were told the "plan is in place and they will have to make it work." In this defining response, the teacher's critical statements about the reform plan were silenced. New objectives became the focus and teachers redefined their understandings about their purpose.

The New Hampshire State Department of Education also organized community meetings for classroom teachers and citizens to attend and voice their concerns to department representatives. The purpose of these meetings was to include teachers and interested citizens who were not members of state committees in reform dialogue (New Hampshire Department of Education, 1997). The State Department of Education sent out flyers to all districts identifying times and locations of these meetings. Individual districts were left to distribute this information to local schools and the community. A teacher who was part of this opportunity at the state level described the purpose of these meetings and the lack of public awareness:

> I know the state definitely wants teacher input if they are concerned about what is happening. They welcome teachers. Now there are meetings set up for teachers and regular community people to talk about the reform plan — to voice their concerns and to ask questions. These sessions aren't very publicized so a lot of people don't know there is a meeting happening. But they are open to the public. (03-3-99)

In the early planning stages, teachers were invited in their individual states to participate in the design of the state tests. As federal policy has gained national momentum the authority of teachers has diminished. An example comes from a teacher who sits on a state test content committee. He describes political changes regarding teacher control over test questions:

> There has been a big change since I first sat on this committee. Now the Department of Education and the legislature are saying there are too many teachers on this committee, which is very strange because one of the ideas was that teachers would be represented. The legislature has said that teachers will design a test that makes us look good and that it truly won't be testing kids. They say we have a vested interest in how end results look. So maybe we shouldn't be the ones writing the questions. So, it is in response to that fear they opened up the committee to other people. Our last meeting was very frustrating because we had people with no education background, and interest groups opposed to what we had done. We did not finish the task we had to do in the amount of time we had with the consultant. So they (the consultants) had to complete the project themselves in what normally would have been a committee task. (03-2-17)

I asked this teacher why he thought there was a growing resistance to recognizing teachers' expertise in education policy decisions:

I think it is that faction of people who mistrust teachers. I think they are the same group that wants merit pay, and feels if a teacher isn't doing a good job by their estimation, fire them. If they do a good job, which now means high test scores, then pay them. I think they think teaching is black and white, cut and dried. They really don't understand what we do. I see the state respond to these fears rather than make people understand what is really going on and try to educate them. (03-3-16, 28)

A State Department of Education representative confirmed the teacher's conclusions:

Yes, there are feelings out there that the test is too influenced by teachers who want to control the results. So now committee membership has expanded so people who want to have a say in it, can have it. That's really better. This way people can't say it's all controlled by teachers. We think it makes the test stronger. (06-2-4)

Teachers described their attempts to respond to state assessments as limited and controlled by power holders and policy designers who determined how and when teachers could participate, offer feedback, and question the components of the reform package. In cases where teachers were identified specifically as contributing to the test design, their authority has diminished as national consultants and citizens with their own political agendas have gained further control.

TEACHERS AND STATE POLITICS: THE POLITICIANS ARE CLUELESS ABOUT WHAT IS ACTUALLY HAPPENING . . .

Teachers also talked about the state legislatures and state education agencies in terms of not understanding what teachers do or how these reform measures were actually affecting them and their students. In interview discussions, classroom teachers described a sense of distrust regarding state-level motives and a lack of support for their work.

The State Department of Education has to look like they are doing something so they turn on the teachers. When they meet with our superintendents or principals, they always come back telling us we have to do more with less. And I think it is because they want to make sure they look like they have a plan to improve things. I say, "Just come and spend a day in my classroom and really see everything that I do." No one has done that—not once. Wouldn't you think if they are going to make decisions for us, they should at least show up at some schools and get an idea about what is happening? (10-1-115)

When you listen to them talk, you know they are clueless about what is happening in our classrooms. They have their procedures and what they have decided has to be done. But what that looks like in an actual classroom is a different matter. They totally wash their hands of that. They say, "Well, you are the experts—just get it done." (03-02-89)

One teacher who is also a state-level union representative described reform as a political action and explained teachers had to deal with it in that context:

The fact is this is a political agenda that has been advanced for political reasons. The only real power is to become politically involved but teachers don't want to go that route. So the other option is to bring their concerns to their union executive boards. Where it would go, frankly, isn't far because honestly, they don't really have any authority, either. This is now the law and you have to deal with it. (03-4-40)

Teachers in this study agreed that trying to become "politically involved" was not a practical option although all agreed it is probably needed. Teachers described time and opportunity limitations that curtailed the kind of activism that would be needed to impact state politics:

One of the problems with this profession is that there is very limited time without students. We just don't have a lot of time to go to the capital and lobby. The National Education Association doesn't seem to think there is a problem and is not speaking for teachers. So I think it is an added burden in our profession. The ones who could best describe the problems and needs are too busy to do it and the ones who should be representing us are ignoring the reality of what is happening. (03-1-105)

We are just trying to do our jobs. We don't have much time to lobby the legislature. The truth is we can't find subs for sick teachers not to mention trying to get subs so we can travel to the capitol and talk with them. We are
just trying to help kids learn what they need to learn in a short amount of
time. We don't have time to be politicians, too. (11-1-32)

Throughout this research, teachers repeatedly concluded that their departments of education and their state legislatures did not support them
and were not interested in what they were experiencing in the reform
changes. They also did not feel they had the time or resources to rely on
traditional political paths of lobbying or public debate to express their
frustration or concerns. Most revealing was that they did not feel they
could change the current course of education reform even if they did have
the time and resources to follow political venues for change.

I asked teachers what they would say if they could talk to their commissioner of education. From state to state, their answers were remarkably
similar.

Actually, there are two things. First, we need an alternative school for the
severely disruptive kids so we don't have to take care of them for even a
month in our classrooms. I think most teachers, especially in this building,
would agree with that. The second thing has to do with time. We need more
time. The elementary teachers need more preparation time. We need more
time to do what we need to do. And part of the reason we lose time is all of
the meetings we have to attend. Meetings for teams, meetings for kids, and
meetings for training to teach things like dental hygiene and a zillion things
that have nothing to do with our curriculum. Plus all of the duties that take
away from time we could spend with our real jobs . . . and dealing with all
of the problems so many kids have. You know, that takes a lot of time. So I
would say, address time and appropriate placement for these very troubled
kids. (11-1-27)

Another teacher reflected on the negative image that the public has
about education and asked the commissioner to advocate for the teaching
profession.

I think the one thing I would ask the people who are in high-profile positions is to really advocate for our profession. I'm not talking about "rah-
rahing" once a year, but talking about the dedication and commitment of

teachers and the good things that are happening. Yes, there are things that go wrong and need improvement and newspapers are more than happy to share that information with the communities. I feel people in leadership roles have to talk about the real issues facing schools like poverty, family violence, child neglect, and the limited resources schools have to address them. We should be recognizing how hard teachers work to compensate for these problems and our struggles and successes in helping students and their families in real ways. People never hear about these things and they are constant events in our schools. (03-3-0-101)

The teachers wanted their state departments of education and the federal government to know about the real problems they are facing every day. They would ask for broader public awareness of the complexity of the children in their classrooms. They would ask for policy makers to take the time to establish a clearer understanding of what is needed to support students with learning and emotional needs and how that impacts a mainstream classroom. They would ask policy makers to respect their authority and include them in policy design. Teachers would like to provide ongoing feedback on what is working and what is not working in the current reform policies and they would like to have an active role in revisions.

TEACHERS AND UNIONS

Teachers are represented by two unions. The first and oldest is the National Education Association (NEA). The second union is the American Federation of Teachers (AFT). Both unions have state chapters and local representation on the district level.

The state teachers' unions are most known for their traditional advocacy role in "bread and butter" issues involving wage and benefit disputes. A typical example of this is a school district in Minnesota that was caught in a contract dispute. The union worked on behalf of teachers during contract negotiations. Tied into local control, town residents publicly debated whether or not to meet the demands of the union contract. A union executive passionately described the union's response to these controversies:

The school board is turning teachers into ping-pong balls! The emotional factor is so important for teachers. How are they supposed to feel when people

come together and say, "Teachers don't deserve higher pay! They only work
nine months out of the year and that includes all of those vacations!" These
people don't know that teachers work on other things in the summer. They
don't see what teachers are up against in the classroom everyday. They don't
see the altruism. They cut the underbelly of the teachers. They are humiliated
in front of the town and then they are supposed to show up on Monday morn-
ing and be enthused about their jobs and the community they work for. People actually don't understand why the teachers are so mad! (07-1-32)

In a "labor" context, the union representative advocated for teachers in
an aggressive posture of addressing injustice and worker rights. The union
is seen as having a legitimate authority to participate in these conversations. This relationship has provided much-needed support for teachers on
highly sensitive salary disputes within their communities. It has also contributed to limited perceptions on how the public evaluates the work of
teachers.

Education theorists Mitchell and Keerchner (1983) describe four work
structures—labor, craft, profession, and art—as defining public perceptions of a worker. Public perception most often aligns labor forces with
union representation. For teachers, union representation creates an association with work that is seen as "rationalized, pre-planned, routine, and directed through inspection and monitoring" (p. 17). Viewed as part of the
general workforce, teachers are viewed as fighting for traditional union
concerns of wages, work conditions, and benefits, which is often the case.
This public perception weakens the professional stance of teachers and di-
minishes their arguments and authority related to professional discretion
and control of decision making in their classrooms.

In contrast to advocacy for wages, the union has assumed a partnership
role with states in its interpretation of reform policy. As partners, the
union has historically had little authority or power over specific teacher
concerns connected with state reform. Unlike the militant tone taken on
wage disputes, the unions have approached many of the reform initiatives
in a tone of conciliation and collaboration with the various state agendas.
A union official in New Hampshire described how their organization interprets state testing:

Those decisions are definitely impacting curriculum in the schools. We
originally fought that kind of testing. But now we see it as giving schools a

kind of benchmark. They are indicators for schools on what they need to strengthen—what they need to improve. (07-1-16)

State teachers' unions have also supported the decision to redefine teacher competencies in terms of state curriculum guidelines. A union representative described how they perceived their role as one of helping teachers to meet the new standards:

> We are working on a mechanism for anticipating big issues that are coming down and helping people deal with them. Now we are reacting to our own curriculum guidelines and student assessment program and one of our goals would be to help teachers to figure out how to interpret test results and work together—to do work collaboratively. It is very big right now for teachers to be able to study test results and adjust curriculum to match test questions. This involves teachers being able to actually be teaching kids the things they need to know to succeed on the state tests. (07-3-37-38)

In a posture of "helping" teachers to know how to respond to test results, the union assists by guiding them along the path of writing curriculum to match test questions. The union promotes full cooperation with the idea of "teaching to the test."

It is at this point where teachers might look to education leaders to suggest analyzing test scores not only for better test results but also to entertain the validity of the testing content, the accuracy of the results in conjunction with other measurements, and the unique circumstances of specific student populations. In a follow-up conversation with the same union representative, the opportunity for critical analysis and discussion was limited and discouraged:

> Now how do you make the best constructive use of reforms so you are not feeling that you are teaching to the test? That, I think, is where the union really could help, in terms of getting people together discussing it—getting the sort of "bitching and moaning" behind us—off the table, and then saying, "How can we make constructive use of this so you are not saying I have to teach to the test but you are using the test results to help you help inform the way you teach?" This could help in grade-level and schoolwide decisions. It's not a union decision. We don't have any control over state tests. But I do feel that the union could help in suggesting ways of collaborating so people feel that they have a voice in all of this. So it's not all administrator driven. (07-2-43)

The union, in partnership with the state reform plans, interprets their role of teacher advocacy as providing ways for teachers to adapt. Teachers who might disagree with reform objectives are seen as "bitching and moaning," sentiments to get off the table. In this orientation, the union does not provide a forum for pedagogical discussion and debate for the teachers it represents. The union defines constructive use of teacher time in terms of collaborative efforts to write curriculum that supports the test.

TEACHERS AND PROFESSIONAL DIALOGUE: THE PEOPLE WHO ARE LISTENING AREN'T THE RIGHT PEOPLE . . .

Opportunities to meet as professionals and discuss ways to interpret change or how to deal with the effects of this change were very limited for teachers in this study. They feel they are left with virtually no time for reflection or problem solving as they struggle with increased time constraints and expanded student and curricular requirements:

When do we get together to talk about these things? Are you kidding? When are we supposed to get together and talk about this? We can barely meet to talk about curriculum and test scores. It is one long race from September to June and all we meet about is how to do it faster and get better scores. (01-3-129)

We aren't involved in decisions about change because we are just too busy. There is no time to sit down and talk like professionals and to organize our thoughts. (01-4-5)

People would definitely like to talk about all of this. But I don't know how they would do that. We are so overscheduled with meetings when we're not teaching that it would be tough to find time. Also, [voice lowers] people don't want to start any trouble. (02-2-11)

The executive director of one of the teachers' unions agreed that scheduling constraints are a national problem for teachers and the limitations for professional dialogue are a serious deterrent for teacher input on reform policy:

What you are hearing from teachers is accurate. They do not have time for reflection and discussion. There is no opportunity to even consider new approaches to time use, lesson planning, or culture change. They are constantly on the run. Unlike teachers in other countries who spend half of their day in planning sessions and the other half actually teaching, our teachers are burdened with a full day of teaching, then rushed to team meetings, faculty meetings, or parent meetings all at the end of the day. On occasion, there might be a half-day workshop but that isn't for professional dialogue. Those times are for trying to hold the system together. (07-1-28)

Additionally, teachers describe tensions between themselves, administrators, and parents that strain mutual understandings and mutually beneficial dialogue:

The people who are listening aren't the right people. People who are listening are those of us in the classroom who can see what is happening. The administration has its own problems worrying about what the district office wants and then there are the "high-powered" parents. They think the classroom should be primarily set up to serve the needs of their child. Parents don't understand that we only have limited teaching time and we have to make the most of that time. And you need to cover more material than ever before with students who have more problems than ever before. Do I think that message is being heard? No, I think people know as much as the newspaper prints which is generally negative. People think teachers are lazy and just want to sit back and watch kids play. They have no idea what is happening in those classrooms. (03-3-87)

Teachers describe feeling pulled by many conflicting and changing forces that limit and define their authority to speak frankly. Faced with precarious support from administrators, the state, and their union, teachers see themselves as "out on a limb" with no control or power over interpretation of reform or critical analysis of its effects.

We are at the will of so many people. We have parents on one end and administration on the other. We aren't sure if administration will back us or not if a parent comes at one of us. So we are "out on a limb" most of the time. I think because we represent so much change in society, people tend to be involved in schools more than any other place. This is where values are and we have to either teach them or stay away from them depending on the politics at that time. We talk about it or ignore it. I have been teaching for 16 years and what we can say and not say just keeps changing and it keeps coming from every direction. We are really out in an open field. We have no control over changes. We have no authority or firm footing. We have no way to say, "Look, this shows that we have made a difference in this child's life. This shows that we have done a good job." It's just about one set of test scores, now. Test scores are very limited in what they tell the public and they are very deceiving. Nobody realizes that except the teachers. (03-7-44)

TEACHERS AND THE "BIG STICK"

Classroom teachers are cast in the role of interpreters of federal guidelines, state mandates, and district plans to meet reform agendas. They are assigned the task of redesigning curriculum and instructional strategies that reflect federal and state curriculum standards and state assessment criteria. Questions of *why* it is happening and *what* must be done have been decided for them. The teacher's role is to determine *how* to do it. Their success is quantifiably measured in their students' test scores. The weight of public perceptions, district evaluation, and state interpretations all rest on how well teachers can interpret and teach to the reform plan handed down to them.

Teachers are very reluctant to challenge these changes in their profession. Powerful enforcements are incorporated in the reform design to promote teacher attitudes of affinity with the change initiatives. Teachers who might try to express questions of "why" or "what" have limited opportunities to be heard and risk estrangement from the professional community. Additionally, teachers who don't cooperate face public scrutiny over test results and jeopardize school support in their communities. The effects of a "big stick" are most certainly felt in these tensions of federal authority and control. It is critical for districts' financial survival that classroom teachers assume a role of compliance and support of state reform initiatives. Powerful incentives of local, state, and federal funding depend upon their performance. Classroom teachers have no alternative but to implement reform initiatives as they are told to do.

Early definitions of what needed to be changed in education policy did not include the perspective of classroom teachers. Caught in the forces of state economic upheaval and crisis in educational funding, the classroom teacher became the object of reform scrutiny and redefinition as political traditions of local school control abdicated authority to state and federal policy design. Teachers were not invited to participate until the reform plan was formulated and its focus and goals were established. They became designers of test questions and contributors toward curriculum frameworks goals under the guidance and supervision of national consultants and state officials. Teachers did not participate in conversations about the value of the curriculum frameworks, how specific curricula were chosen, or what standardized curriculum continuums would mean when adapted to the diversity of learning needs in the classroom. Rather, teachers participated in standardized curriculum definitions and regulation of curriculum continuums that supported the economic agendas of the business community.

The state assessment is a powerful regulator of teacher autonomy. Investigation in this study uncovered severe and costly repercussions and implications for classroom teachers if their students test poorly. Test scores are used to define the quality and confirm the value of the work of teachers. Poor test scores are linked to ineffective teaching, which translates into failing schools. State controls are put in place to monitor these results and determine state-level action through district plans, the retraining of teachers, and state-level discretionary allocation of state and federal funds. Teachers have not been a part of the conversations that formed these interpretations of the state assessment. Instead, they are the focus of interpretation through state report cards and public disclosure of student test scores.

Official state rhetoric included teachers in all levels of reform definition. Teachers described their actual participation as each of these levels was explored. Teachers who participated in the early committee work felt a sense of contribution and significance in what they accomplished. The state, their districts, and their union identified these teachers as leaders in the profession. As test design was refined, the same teachers described a lessening of their authority on these decisions as interpreters of political forces began questioning teachers' motives in designing test questions that might be "too easy" or would benefit teachers' own struggles with accountability based on students' test scores.

In these cases where the state provided opportunities for teacher participation, powerful authorities determined how much "participating" would occur. Researcher Angus (1994, in Smyth, 1989) describes this as "background power" through which levels of participation are defined:

> Although the cooperation of diverse participants is to be invited by transformative, purposing, or visionary leadership, the participation is to be shaped quite blatantly in this perspective by the larger-than-life leader. But the influence upon participation of the ideological context and background power relationships within which such channeled participation is invited, is overlooked. (p. 83)

Authorities in this study argued that participants in state reform had the freedom to interpret their own degree of support to its goals. They claimed teachers could always come forward and express concerns. In these same districts, teachers described a force that was often subtle but clearly showed itself in the ways teachers did *not* challenge district authorities. Educational researcher Lukes (1974) in his analysis of power explains, "The most effective and insidious use of power is to prevent such conflict from arising in the first place" (p. 23). He clarified the purpose of this kind of power is to "prevent people to whatever degree, from having grievances by shaping perceptions, cognitions, and preferences in such a way that they accept their role in the existing order of things, either because they can see or imagine no alternative to it, or because they see it as natural and unchangeable" (p. 24).

My observation is that teachers in this study were silent because of their limited awareness of or limited opportunities to express any authority in issues of federal and state reform. As a result, their participation was minimal and ineffective. Further, this lost opportunity has deadened teachers' sense of professionalism, stifled creativity, and fostered resentment and antagonism toward authorities. These effects are not only damaging to teachers who must comply, but also for students who must learn under heightened pressures and tensions in the classroom.

In addition to reform plan strategies to force the compliance of teachers, powerful and enforcing sentiments are described by all levels of authority to ensure the appearance of teacher consensus. Teachers are categorized by their receptivity to the established definitions of reform. Cooperative teachers are identified with the collective group of power holders. Nameless teachers who don't cooperate are characterized with undesirable personal qualities and risk the consequences of collegial estrangement and public disapproval. By censoring critique, participation in reform conversation is left for those who express attitudes supportive of reform objectives and who take on the appearance of speaking for the majority. Enforcements are designed to ensure teacher compliance through professional evaluation, district plans, and public disclosure of student test scores. The work of teachers is monitored under these many layers of control. Education theorist Giroux (1988) portrays teachers grappling with reform as "being trapped in an apparatus of domination that works with all of the certainty of a Swiss watch" (p. xxxi).

IV

The Future of Reform: Promises That Can Be Kept

8

Classroom Teachers and the Future of Reform

Classroom teachers who participated in this study supported the need for education reform. They agree with the importance of identifying curricula that can support the needs of an academically competent and independent adult population. They affirm the value of assessment in measuring student success as well as its significance as one indicator of their own success in meeting learning objectives. Additionally, teachers share with state-level policy makers and the general public the concern that not all teachers are competent teachers. They endorse limiting teaching certification to only those people who demonstrate pedagogical skills that are essential to effective teaching. Teachers also expressed the need for professional development opportunities that support and improve their work. In each of the conversations, my data showed agreement between teachers, their unions, government agencies, and the business sector that there is a need to examine education policy, evaluate systems, and prescribe change that includes accountability measures.

Classroom teachers do not agree with their state reform designs. They do not feel they were represented in early conversations in which state policy makers assumed authority over what needed to be changed or how changes would be defined. Teachers became implementers of an established reform plan after these fundamental decisions were made. This chapter begins with analysis and critique of the structure of the reform plan and underlying assumptions made by its designers about teachers, their students, and standardized instruction.

CLASSROOM TEACHERS AND THE STRUCTURE OF REFORM

The business community sounded the original alarm for a sweeping education reform movement. The meaning of schooling was expanded to include serving the economic needs of the state. Based in scientific or "systems" language, the business community presented the solutions for school improvement in terms of the "production" of specific "outcomes" with concepts of efficiency, economic functionalism, and bureaucratic monitoring systems as tools to reach these goals. In a sense, schools took on a factory model with an input-output design that defined students at the start of the school year as raw material and test results as the finished product.

An input-output model includes identification of what the "input" is, how the processing mechanisms operate, what controls are used to measure quality, and what the desired "output" or product will look like. The national reform plan starts with the significant assumption that all children come to school equally receptive and able to learn. The "input" of the reform plan is curriculum standards and guidelines. This "high-status" knowledge is preestablished information everyone needs to know. The teacher can be compared to the machine that processes the input of knowledge in a manner that results in the measurable outcomes or output. The tool to measure this output is the state assessment. The system of state and federal monitoring of student assessments establishes quality control over teachers' work.

The reform plan assumes formal authority over schools. The work of teachers is rationalized and mechanized into a process in which teachers follow standardized curricula and students meet certain learning objectives at specific times in a learning continuum. Learning improvement is verified through careful monitoring of assessment results and teacher competency requirements. The authors of the reform plan have projected increased teacher productivity and improved student learning as ultimately answering the original call by the business community for a prepared workforce and a stable economy.

While these promises are enticing, the simplistic approach presents a limited understanding of the complexities of the system it is intended to reform. Inherent in the problems of design and structure of the reform package, are the fundamental assumptions made by policy designers about what schools can realistically accomplish, the promised benefits of standardized curriculum, and the authority given to standardized tests as reliable indicators of student learning and teacher competency.

ASSUMPTIONS BY AUTHORITIES IN STATE REFORM

The federal reform plan is based on several assumptions that are erroneous in application. First is the assumption that teachers, when properly regulated, can correct the problems in education. Researchers have suggested that this assumption has led the public to unreasonable expectations of teachers and school. Sarason (1990) explains:

> To a significant degree, the major educational problems stem from the fact that educators not only accepted responsibility for schooling, but, more fatefully, also adopted a stance that essentially said, "We know how to solve and mange the problems of schools in America." Educators did not say, "There is much we do not know, many problems that are intractable to our efforts, and many individuals we are not reaching or helping." Put another way, educators were not calling attention to what was obvious to them in their daily work. (p. 37)

Sarason further explains how the research community also contributed to this assumption:

> The researcher, like the educational practitioner, wrestles with unknowns, trying to do his or her best with extraordinarily complex problems. Like the practitioners, the educational researchers promised the public more than they could deliver, implicitly suggesting a time table that was wildly unrealistic. Far from seeing his kinship with the practitioner, the educational researcher tended to use the practitioner as a scapegoat. And all the while, both researcher and practitioner knew in their hearts they were seeking their ways through a forest of ignorance that seemed to grow trees faster than they could be cut down. (p. 38)

Teachers describe societal realities that impact their efforts in the classroom. They see many of these problems as endemic in society. The many children who come to school with emotional and social issues so pressing that learning is impeded are of specific concern. Issues of family breakdowns, chemical and substance abuse, child neglect, and effects of domestic and social violence were just a few of the daily influences that teachers have no control over but profoundly affect the motivation and focus of children in the learning process. Additionally, teachers describe parents who do not understand or support their work. These parents, in some cases, actually work against teachers' efforts. Reform intentions do not alter these realities.

A second assumption in reform design is that state standards provide the right objectives for all students. Teachers' success is measured in terms of following the established curriculum guidelines. In No Child Left Behind (NCLB) policy, teachers are recognized as capable of and responsible for designing effective instruction but they are not given the authority to first identify what *is* appropriate curriculum or *when* it should be taught. Teachers in this study described grave consequences of this reasoning. In many cases, teachers identified students who weren't ready for the prescribed curriculum on predetermined timelines. Instruction for these children became meaningless and counterproductive as they faced compounded failure progressively through their school years. For others, the pacing was too fast and resulted in minimal understanding of content with little or no opportunity for remediation or review. For all students, meaningful connections between curricular areas were infrequent as teachers were forced to focus on specific topics and segmented learning blocks to "stay on schedule" and conform to test design. Effective lesson design is severely compromised in these contradictions. The addition of teacher development opportunities to improve implementation of state standards does not solve the problem of curriculum that is inappropriate for some students in the first place.

Teachers describe the problems with controlled objectives and the reality of a highly diverse student population with many different learning needs as a source of frustration and growing dissatisfaction with their work. Teachers feel "deskilled" as they review what they are capable of doing being compromised by what they feel they *must* do to stay on track with guidelines. The authority of teachers to adapt curriculum to the learning needs of students is limited. Rushed instruction to meet preset testing timelines restrains efforts to teach in more interesting ways. Veteran teachers refer to their knowledge and experience as no longer valued or even applicable to the methods they are now required to adopt. Teachers feel that the quality of their instruction is downgraded to yield immediate results that reflect minimal standards of achievement geared only for the fortunate students who come to school "on grade level" and ready to learn.

Teachers' conclusions are confirmed by education researchers who have examined the effects of standardized curriculum on teaching. Mc-Neil (1988) reports standardized efforts as "dumbing down" teachers:

> These top-down reforms not only ignore many of the dynamics that produce low-quality instruction, but they actually reinforce them. By applying across-the-board generic remedies, they are dumbing down the best teaching even as they try to raise the bottom. Disclaimers that these will establish "minimums" have little credibility when the best teachers are the ones who feel most alienated and who are talking of leaving.
>
> Good teaching cannot be engineered into existence. But an engineering approach to schooling can crowd out good teaching. Instead of holding up a variety of models for practice and learning from strengths, these reforms continue our historically flawed search for "one best way" to run our schools. These reforms take a cynical view of teachers' abilities to contribute constructively to schooling; they choose to make the content, the assessment of students, and the decisions about pedagogy all teacher-proof, so that a standardized model will become the norm. (p. 485)

A third assumption underlying the reform structure is that the state assessment tool can accurately confirm student achievement and can indicate teacher competency. Teachers do not see the current assessment tool as an accurate measurement of either of these goals. Rather, they describe the state assessment as promoting decreased learning for their students and a loss of professional credibility for themselves. These alarming conclusions are illustrated in teachers' descriptions of an overemphasis on "high-stakes" test scores that deflected the teachers' focus on the work of improving instruction and learning based on the actual needs of the students. Rather than increasing the amount of material being covered, teachers describe "dropping" content because it's not on the test. In its place, teachers describe new teaching objectives that focus strictly on state content and "one right answer" instruction in preparation for the test format. When these practices are employed, in-depth coverage of content is replaced with minimal and superficial understandings for students.

The state assessment is used to ensure greater teacher competency and increased student learning. Teachers claim it is having the opposite effect. With the pressure of state assessments tests as the primary indicator of achievement for students and teachers, success or failure for everyone is determined on the basis of one consideration—did the scores go up? Information about actual student knowledge is incomplete and conclusions about achievement are misleading. Rather than promoting greater teacher competency, the power of assessment results limit and control the expertise of teachers.

It is assumed that the state assessments can also provide an accurate understanding to the public about each district's success in reaching high academic standards. Additionally, it is assumed that test results will offer all citizens an accurate picture of comparisons between districts through public disclosure of scores. The effects of communities having limited insight into what test scores actually represent have been devastating for some schools and some neighborhoods. Under these pressures, questionable and sometimes unethical practices have occurred in schools as a means to survive public humiliation and funding backlash. Investigation described in preceding chapters indicates that some districts are responding to pressures of public disclosure in aggressive ways directed at children and teachers to ensure favorable comparisons. Teachers describe examples of test score manipulation through test preparation procedures as now common, with no concern for the authentic instructional time that is lost every year in these efforts.

In a study done by Cohn and Kottkamp (1993) on "control by testing," the effects of testing procedure were examined in cases where the test results were interpreted as the conclusive indicator of teacher and student success:

> It obscured the built-in tension between learning and control by masquerading as the great impetus for learning, when in reality it was the most refined form of control—mystifying and reifying achievement and learning into figures on wall charts. The numbers carried none of the reality of their begetting: hours of teaching for the tests, absence of motivation in those whose learning they purport to measure with validity, and the quite rational pollution that results when the only rule in the game is "Score high!" (p. 214)

Assessment results provide an accurate picture of which districts have the money, resources, and student population to score well on state tests. Wealthier districts with access to more support staff and teacher training resources to incorporate state curriculum standards into school curriculum have a distinct advantage over districts that cannot afford these efforts. Fiscal inequities are most apparent in these struggles to compete for funding. Districts starting out with the most wealth have the greatest chance of increased public support and increased funding. It is perhaps the greatest irony of the reform plan that districts which have the low test scores are penalized by losing funding that could help them raise their scores.

PROMISES THAT CANNOT BE KEPT

Despite almost 20 years of national focus, we remain working with a nationally established reform agenda that cannot meet its promises. Even in cases where teachers can rewrite their curricula to fit exact assessment content and procedures, districts cannot guarantee uniform assessment results, or, more importantly, that the learning needs of all students will be met. The reality remains that students are complex human beings who come to school with a wide range of abilities, experiences, and cultural factors that cannot be addressed in a one-size-fits-all curriculum or assessment package. Designing a reform package that is based on assumptions that do not address actual diversity and challenges of the classroom cannot succeed for teachers, their students, or the community calling for competent graduates.

The legal rights of those students who do not meet the state-promised levels of achievement also present serious potential consequences. A disconcerting question arises: What are the states' responsibilities for the child who *does* get left behind? Kirst and Guthrie (1994) provide some thought-provoking questions:

> Build a curriculum ballpark and lawyers will come. Whatever the other merits or demerits of national curriculum and performance standards, they assuredly will serve as anchor points against which to judge the adequacy and equity of a state's education system. If a state adopts a performance standard and Johnny's reading does not achieve that standard, is the state at risk for malpractice? If the state submits a standardized curriculum package to the U.S. Secretary of Education, which is then approved, every school or district in the state better ensure that it offers such courses and experiences. Otherwise, Johnny has a strong equal protection case. (pp. 169–170)

Policy makers have failed to realize that the establishment of goals that are unattainable for some constituents has implications that go beyond controls of accountability for teachers. Standardized curriculum and assessment have also established accountability responsibilities for state education departments to provide uniform *opportunity* for all students as well as uniform results. By their design, standardized curriculum and regulated assessments limit what those opportunities will be.

CLASSROOM TEACHERS' RECOMMENDATIONS FOR TRUE REFORM

Teachers, policy makers, and the community are united in a common goal of improved educational opportunity for all students. Central in redefinitions of the classroom teachers' role in reform is the examination and reinterpretation of decision making and authority over the work of teachers. Methods of measuring success must be reexamined and teacher accountability must be designed to reflect the true diversity and complexity of today's classroom. Teachers are not looking for a relaxing of standards or clearly defined objectives. A loss of curriculum guidelines or performance standards would result in fragmented objectives and inconsistent opportunities for children. Rather, teachers propose a collaborative process that includes administrators, the community, state and federal policy makers, and teachers.

For attainable reform to occur, new understandings are required that can support authentic change. First, teaching and learning must be redefined in terms of meaningfulness and relevancy to children in the real classroom setting. Second, time must be examined and redefined as a resource rather than a barrier to education goals. Third, power relationships must be redefined to ensure a place for teachers to safely discuss the ongoing work of reform. In a framework of shared authority, reform conversation can begin about the processes of curriculum identification, instructional procedure, meaningful assessment interpretation, and authority in decision making.

LEARNING AS MEANINGFUL INTERACTION

Teachers in this study spoke about their sense of disconnection with the curriculum controls they are forced to implement in their classrooms.

They talked about the difficulties they face in motivating students who don't see relevancy in the material or feel success in their learning. They feel the curriculum they offer is too often not at the level many of their students need. It is disturbing that teachers describe their students as more diverse and complex than ever before while stating they have never been more controlled in how they can respond.

Classroom teachers describe working with the developmental needs of their students as essential to effective instruction. Further, teachers argue that their attention to the whole child includes the social, moral, and personal dimensions that support cognitive development. An important consideration is that curricular material has relevance in the lives of the children from diverse communities. Teachers contrast the current "test-driven" approach to learning against a "student-driven" approach based on the developmental and cognitive readiness of the students who are actually in the classroom.

Lieberman and Miller (1990) describe effective teaching strategies that were very different from what teachers are currently practicing:

> Teaching and learning are interdependent, not separate functions. In this view, teachers are primarily learners. They are problem posers and problem solvers; they are researchers; and they are intellectually engaged in unraveling the learning process both for themselves and for the young people in their charge. Learning is not consumption; it is knowledge production. Teaching is not performance; it is facilitative leadership. Curriculum is not given; it is constructed empirically, based on emergent needs and interests of learners. Assessment is not judgment; it is documents of progress over time. Instruction is not technocratic; it is inventive, craft-like, and above all, an imperfect enterprise. (p. 12)

Researchers view students as active participants in the learning process. Teachers are facilitators engaged in methodology that promotes active engagement, exploration, and discovery. Curriculum design reflects objectives that are relevant to students' lives with goals that are achievable. Teachers in this study concur with these findings. They describe methods recommended by researchers as left to those few remaining moments of discretionary teaching. They need the professional autonomy to apply teaching strategies and lesson design in ways that meet the actual needs of their students.

Teachers describe the importance of achievable learning goals and authentic accomplishments in the learning process. This kind of instruction begins with an understanding of each student's readiness to learn and where he or she is located on a content continuum. It is this information that defines attainable goals and provides a framework for instructional strategies. Teachers support curriculum frameworks through this process. They value the consistency and structure of a progression of skills and knowledge. The problem for teachers is the regulation and control that comes with a standardized format geared to grade-level specifications. Teachers need the autonomy to identify the appropriate instructional levels for their students, review and remediate as necessary, and promote students to next levels after mastery is achieved.

Teachers need the flexibility to make curricular adjustments based on students' responses. They describe the loss of "teachable moments" in which curiosity shifts attention to the exploration of related topics. It is during these times that students find connections between curricular areas and application to their real-life experiences. This supports meaningful connections between academics and the interests and lives of the students. Teachers want the professional discretion to provide opportunities for spontaneity, exploration, and active student participation in the learning process.

Teachers link meaningful learning to meaningful assessment. They agree with and support methods of assessing student achievement. They also value an assessment tool that promotes the flexibility to adjust their instruction. Teachers described two kinds of assessment tools that they see as relevant to their work. First, a tool that is diagnostic and prescriptive in design and interpretation is needed. Tests of this nature are administered at the start of the school year rather than at the end. Such a tool measures what students know, where skills are weak, and what direction teachers should take to teach to achievement. This kind of assessment tool provides a profile about each student and provides relevant baseline information for academic short-term and long-term learning objectives and goals.

Second, teachers support achievement tests that follow prescriptive instruction. These tests measure student levels of understanding based on mastery objectives. Teachers argue that meaningful assessment must also carry intrinsic value for students and parents if its interpretation is to be valid and its costs justified. Teachers strongly recommend shifting from the current practice of yearly testing based on grade-level standards to yearly testing of actual academic progress for each child. A "growth model" of testing measures the advancements each child makes based on his/her skills and knowledge at the start of the school year. This change requires a reexamination of the purpose of state assessments, what they are meant to indicate, and how they align with reform intentions.

Teachers' competency is currently tied directly into state achievement tests. Data from this study and other studies cited indicate that this control strategy has defeated the original purposes of the state assessments. Instead, it has created pressures that have led to test score pollution. Teachers report that test training has replaced classroom instruction. The integrity of the test has been compromised and any value that could come from testing is limited. While the state assessments do show how well students take the state assessments, they do not provide a reliable measure of student progress. Teachers feel that the connection between teacher competency and test scores has created meaningless pressures for students and antagonisms and frustration for teachers.

The purpose of standardized testing must be redefined to provide tools that accurately measure true student achievement while providing valuable data on how to improve instruction and how to best meet the needs of the population being served. The measurement of students, not teachers, is the focus of this model. Teachers are collaborators in the interpretation of test results and designers of curriculum that supports test results. The state assessment becomes one tool that indicates successful instruction and student progress.

When improved understandings about student learning become the reason for assessment, manipulation of test scores becomes counterproductive to testing purposes. Valid test scores are used as tools for teachers to further understand and interpret the progress of their students. Teachers are allowed to objectively analyze and interpret measurable progress and reappraise student-centered objectives. Students benefit from informed understanding of their actual achievement. Under these conditions, the community, school districts, the state, and the federal government are, in fact, given an accurate accounting of each child's progress through the course of a school year. Teacher competencies are measured according to the pedagogical skills brought to the classroom and the expertise demonstrated in lesson design based on student needs.

THE TYRANNY OF TIME

Classroom teachers in this study discussed how they have been "deskilled" by reform initiatives in their attempts to make instruction meaningful and appropriate for their students. Teachers stressed that it isn't that they don't know what to do or how to do it. The single greatest obstacle preventing them from meeting the needs of their students is time. They do not have the time to remediate students who are failing or accelerate instruction for those who are ready. They don't have the time to meet with students individually or engage in interpersonal conversations that are meaningful. Teachers do not have time to meet professionally with colleagues, share expertise, or collaborate with other teachers to integrate instruction. All teachers in this study recognize the importance of these areas of their work. Teachers agreed that their biggest problems are time constraints that prohibit them from doing what they know how to do.

Schools are governed by definitions of time. With few exceptions, schools open and close at fixed times in the day. They operate about nine and a half months out of the year. According to the National Center for Education Statistics (1997) schools typically offer about 5.6 hours of classroom time each day. The norm required for school attendance, according to the Council of Chief State School Officers, is 180 days (National Education Commission on Time and Learning, 1994).

The school day is also regulated by time. Teachers are required to dedicate certain numbers of minutes to curricular areas. Regardless of how complex or simple a school subject is or how well or poorly students understand the concepts, instructional time blocks and assessment schedules drive how material is presented to students and what opportunity they have to comprehend and master it. Schedules are designed to coordinate content teaching with special education support. Students come and go following schedules of integrated arts specialists, physical education classes, and student support services. The bus schedule determines when the day starts and ends. In all cases, bells and clocks, rather than students and teachers, drive every decision on when instruction can begin and when instruction will stop.

Education reform is needed not because teachers are incapable of effective instruction without controls, but rather because the structuring of time in schools prohibits teachers from doing what they are trained to do.

Teachers are working within status-quo-entrenched definitions of what schools do and when they do it that no longer meet the challenges teachers face today. Fundamental definitions of when schools operate and how the school day is structured dramatically limit teachers' options. The reform plan designers did not consider the problem of time when they added standardized instruction and the additional regulations of timelines and assessment schedules to a school day that was already struggling within a system ruled by time controls that impeded learning.

The National Education Commission on Time and Learning (1994) produced a study entitled *Prisoners of Time*. Milton Goldberg, the executive director of the commission, was also the executive director of the National Commission on Excellence in Education that produced *A Nation at Risk* (1983). The commission concluded that not considering the effect of time in the national reform package is the "fundamental design flaw" in its creation:

> Decades of school reform have foundered on a fundamental design flaw, the assumption that learning can be doled out by the clock and defined by the calendar. Research confirms common sense. Some students take three to six times longer than others to learn the same thing. Yet, students are caught in a time trap—processed on an assembly line scheduled to the minute. Our usage of time virtually assures the failure of many students. (p. 2)

Based on a 24-month investigation, the Commission defined five unresolved issues that present "insurmountable barriers" to the efforts of the federal reform program to improve learning. They are similar to the responses of the teachers in this study:

- The fixed clock/calendar prevents learning goals from being met.
- Academic and instructional time has been stolen to make room for a host of nonacademic activities.
- Today's school schedule does not respond to the significant changes that have reshaped American life outside of school.
- Educators do not have the time to do their jobs thoroughly.
- Mastering world-class standards will require more time for almost all students. (pp. 2–6)

Teachers need time to develop effective lessons. They time to assess students in meaningful ways and discuss those results with students and their parents. They need time to talk with students, listen to them, and discuss their progress. They need time to confer with parents in ways that are meaningful and inclusive. They need time to meet with administrators and to receive regular feedback from instructional leaders. And, they need time for professional development: to stay current with professional research and journals, confer with colleagues, and gain from each other's expertise. In these changes, the value of teachers' time is broadened beyond "only when teaching" to include thoughtful preparation that makes teaching effective for children.

If we really are going to improve learning for students, we are going to have to rethink how we organize time. Time as a control in curricular and assessment decisions must be transformed into time as a resource to be used in meeting student objectives. The "time-driven" school day must be reinvented to a "student-centered" school day. Instructional time should be defined in terms of student's abilities, levels of achievement, and academic goals. In this framework, teachers structure time to support the wide range of skills and knowledge students represent in the classroom and they teach in ways that identify student objectives as the driving force in the learning experience.

The framework of the school year and the length of the school day are going to have to be reconsidered. Current assumptions about school calendars and the hours schools are open need to be put in the context of expanding curricular requirements and student populations with a broad range of learning and social needs. Schools that are open all year and building schedules that include flexible before- and after-school programming are starting points for broadened opportunities to meet the changing academic, developmental, and emotional needs of students. Considerations of time and how we use it require further research and evaluation as reinterpretations open the possibilities for schools to meet the needs of students and their communities.

These recommendations would require changes in the very definitions of how schooling is perceived and valued by the public. Some of these changes would require inclusive conversations within districts to assess how current scheduling is determined, what the priorities are, and how rescheduling would look. We cannot begin to act on reform objectives without providing a school structure that allows teachers the time that is needed to prepare, design, implement, and meaningfully assess the work they are asked to do. Other changes would require redefinitions of school hours and the school year. Further staffing and budgeting considerations would be costly. Teachers argue that the effects of current inappropriate and ineffective education are more costly. A better-educated population remains the goal of reform. This effort is pointless if we do not address the stark reality that students cannot achieve reform intentions unless we take a long look at how we are using teachers' time.

CLASSROOM TEACHERS AS
PARTICIPANTS IN REFORM DIALOGUE

The education reform policy is a top-down, uniform, "by-the-numbers" application for change that originated on the federal level. This study has provided descriptions from teachers on the limited and controlled opportunities they had to express concerns about reform design and the effects they were seeing in their classrooms. The reform structure provides little authority or opportunity for teachers to engage in its revision, redefinition of purpose, or evaluation of its worth. Teachers argue that their informed perspective is vital in these interpretations and their observations should be the starting point in reform reauthorization.

Teachers identify serious obstacles in their efforts to achieve appropriate levels of learning for all children. They describe grave consequences of reform regulations for themselves and their students. Their concerns are substantiated by national studies done by researchers and education scholars. Teachers also describe reluctance and fear about voicing these concerns to authorities or decision makers. Teachers' fears were confirmed in interviews I conducted. Teachers were strongly discouraged from expressing concern or challenging the authority of district administrators and state policy makers.

Teachers' knowledge and expertise remain at the borders of federal reform definitions in the current power taxonomy. Teachers' conclusions are set apart from the official perspectives that regulate and control working conditions. Lost from critical conversations are the vital day-to-day realities about students, learning, school structures, and the current assessment practices that resist current reform intentions. The omission of the teachers' perspectives in reform definitions has resulted in a plan that cannot achieve its purpose. The framework of education reform must be changed from teachers being the objects of reform to teachers being coinventers with a renewed focus on students and how they learn. Reform concentration must shift from "how to manage teachers" to how to "better meet the needs of students." This evokes conversations that include shared understandings about students, curriculum design that reflects developmental and cognitive stages, assessment tools that inform instructional decisions, and shared planning with the goal of creating learning environments that are conducive to the needs of students and their families. Education philosopher Maxine Greene (1988) explains that this kind of planning is a joint effort:

> Where freedom is concerned, it is taken to signify either liberation from domination or the provision of spaces where choices can be made. There is a general acknowledgement that the opening of such spaces depends on support and connectedness. It is to interpret from as many vantage points as possible lived experience, the ways there are of being in the world. (p. 120)

Additionally, teachers need to be active partners in the evaluation of reform initiatives. Reform is an evolving idea and relational to changing populations and settings. Teachers must be included in conversations about its effects and be able to make adjustments in its improvement. Discrepancies between espoused beliefs and actions or actions and outcomes must be considered, analyzed for effectiveness, and redefined as purposes change. The evaluation of teachers' work and students' achievement must reflect the actual circumstances of the classroom and the complex work that teachers are doing. Teachers' authority to speak to these issues allows for reinterpretation of goals and alternative approaches that support the dynamics and reality of the classroom.

PROMISES THAT CAN BE KEPT

With greater freedom over curriculum planning and assessment design, teachers have the autonomy to make learning more meaningful and relevant for the majority of their students. Unresolved in the complexity of the classroom dynamics are the needs of those children who come to school with severe social and emotional issues that debilitate their learning and often impact the learning of others. Teachers identify this problem as one they do not have control over and are not receiving adequate support or resources to address. It must be recognized by policy makers and the public that powerful societal forces outside of the classroom directly impact the achievement of many students. Conversations must begin about what realistic expectations are for teachers and these troubled youngsters. Difficult but pertinent questions must be raised, honestly examined, and answered frankly as part of state reform intentions. Can schools promise to deliver the same educational outcomes for every child? Should we stop punishing schools for low achievement and start looking at ways to help them? How do we design a teacher competency measurement that reflects the actual progress of each child each year and also factors in societal forces outside of the teachers' control? How do we establish the boundaries between authentic and attainable educational objectives for students and the school's responsibilities in being a change agent for societal problems in the community? What social services and resources must schools provide to ensure the safety and support of all youngsters and their teachers in today's schools? And, how can the structure of schools and the use of time support rather than resist efforts to meet reform objectives and intentions?

Questions of this nature provide grounding for early discussions about what reform can accomplish. The current quick solutions of increased curriculum and assessment controls are ineffective solutions to these complex issues. Attainable reform objectives require long-term planning that begins with reflective dialogue between teachers, their districts, state and federal authorities, and the communities that pay for and rely on reform integrity.

CONCLUDING POINTS AND RECOMMENDATIONS

A climate of reform has evolved that is not good for teachers or their students. Tactics of finger-pointing, evasion, and political debates on "who is responsible for what' overshadow resourceful problem solving and decision making within professional communities. Reform controls now stifle teacher capabilities. Forced standardized curriculum has paralyzed teachers' creativity and professional expertise. Unilateral mechanized competition between our schools has turned education against itself. Districts are pitted against districts for status or funding. Colleagues suspect colleagues of unethical practices in frantic efforts to meet high-stakes test standards that have questionable validity and are too often compromising actual instructional time for students. Teachers are telling us we must recognize what is happening when students with serious learning and emotional needs are viewed as a detriment to class averages and teachers must decide who is most deserving of their time and skills. The consequences of an education reform policy that has excluded teachers' knowledge and experience in its creation has impacted education in ways that I believe policy makers did not anticipate and educators cannot support.

If real reform is to occur, classroom teachers must be active in defining its objectives, design, implementation, and assessment. Reform as a product handed down to teachers must be redesigned to be a process in which teachers are vital contributors. Understandings between the reality of the classroom and intentions of change must be brought together in a spirit of collaboration and support. Classroom teachers must be actively present in conversations about what is happening in their schools, what is working, and what is defeating their purposes. The benefits of current national reform efforts also need to be identified and salvaged. Changes from the "inside out" rather than the "top down" must be defined to make schools places where authentic learning can occur, progress can be followed, and goals that are achievable and measurable for everyone are set.

Teachers need the authority to participate in defining what a "highly qualified" teacher means and how it is measured. Accountability must be broadened to include skillful interpretation of pedagogical theory and application that suits the learning, developmental, and social needs of students. Meaningful professional development, collegial interaction, and instructional leadership and feedback from administration are required to foster a productive and supportive professional climate. These efforts are essential for the dignity and professional status of educators as well as the personal and academic welfare of students.

We have to take a long, hard look at how we are using instructional time. Teachers are spending too much of the school day taking care of behavior issues and special needs that are outside of the scope of academic instruction. We need to consider if we really want trained educators using their time to monitor lunch rooms or supervising bus duty when they could be using that time to work with students. We have to recognize the instructional time that is being lost every year because teachers stop all instruction for several weeks (and in some cases, months) to prepare for state tests. We have to consider how to structure the school day to maximize teacher-student contact time. We need to provide supports and alternatives for those influences that distract from the learning process.

We need a better way of assessing what students know and determining what they need to know. If we really are trying to compete on a global scale, we must move beyond the current "one right answer" approach to assessment and start looking at ways that measure collaboration, synthesis of knowledge, evaluative summation, and critical analysis. These skills are not achieved by practicing for declarative tests. These conceptual and interaction skills are the result of intentional instruction that includes sufficient time to consider complex ideas and deepen understandings of content. The federal government needs to provide support for these efforts that includes more efficient and authentic testing systems.

I do not suggest that the teachers' stories in this study or the recommendations listed will provide the solutions for the many problems facing education today, nor do I believe opening dialogue between teachers and reform authorities will transform existing tensions surrounding reform interpretations. I do suggest that reform is only possible if teachers are fundamental contributors in determining which changes are needed, what the changes will be, and how the changes will be implemented and assessed.

Starting reform conversation with classroom teachers will not simplify the reform effort. Teachers will address real problems in schools that government and business policy makers have not recognized. The realities of complex social issues, disparate funding, outdated school systems and structuring, insufficient staffing, minimal learning standards, and increased disconnection between teachers and students will challenge the accepted assumptions about what is wrong with schools. Teachers are not the source of these problems. Standardized curriculum and assessment along with additional controls on teachers will not resolve them. Teachers argue that meaningful change cannot occur until we start taking these problems seriously. Realistic education reform must begin with classroom teachers as its definer, not its object. The stakes have never been higher.

References

Apple, M. W. (1990). *Ideology and curriculum.* New York: Routledge.

Armstrong, T. (1994). *Multiple intelligences in the classroom.* Alexandria, VA: Association for Supervision and Curriculum Development.

Arons, S. (1994). The threat to freedom in Goals 2000. In N. Cobb (Ed.), *The future of education: Perspectives on national standards in America* (pp. 55–60). New York: College Board.

Association for Supervision and Curriculum Development. (1986, September). *School reform policy: A call to reason.* Alexandria, VA: Association for Supervision and Curriculum Development.

Atkin, J. (1994). Developing world-class education standards: Some conceptual and political dilemmas. In N. Cobb (Ed.), *The future of education: Perspectives on national standards in America.* (pp. 61–83). New York: College Board.

Ball, S. (1990). *Foucault and education: Disciplines and knowledge.* London: Routledge.

Barthes, R. (1972). *Mythologies.* London: Jonathon Cape.

Belden, Russonello, & Stewart Firm. (2000a). *Raising education standards and assessing results.* Commissioned by The Business Roundtable. Accessed August 28, 2007, from www.businessroundtable.org

Belden, Russonello, & Stewart Firm. (2000b). *Making the grade: Teachers attitudes toward academic standards and state testing.* Survey conducted for *Education Week.* Accessed August 28, 2007, from www.edweek.com

Bentham, J. (1977). The eye of power. In C. Gordon & M. Foucault (Eds.), *Power and knowledge: Selected interviews and other writings* (pp. 152–176). New York: Pantheon.

Berliner, D., & Biddle, B. (1995). *The manufactured crisis: Myths, fraud, and attack on America's public schools.* New York: Addison-Wesley.

Bidwell, C. (1965). The school as a formal organization. In J. G. March (Ed.), *Handbook of organizations* (pp. 972–1020). Chicago: Rand McNally.

Bloom, B. (1980, February). The new direction in educational research: Alterable variables. *Phi Beta Kappan, 67*(1), 21–27.

Blumer, H. (1969). *Symbolic interactionism.* Englewood Cliffs, NJ: Prentice Hall.

Bogdan, R., & Biklen, S. (1992). *Qualitative research for education: An introduction to theory and methods.* Needham Heights, MA: Allyn and Bacon.

Bohlman, L. G., & Deal, T. E. (1991). *Reframing organizations: Artistry, choice, and leadership.* San Francisco: Jossey-Bass.

Bourdieu, P., & Passeron, J. C. (1977). *Reproduction in education, society and culture.* London: Sage.

Boyd, W. L. (1987, Summer). Public education's last harrah? Schizophrenia, amnesia, and ignorance in school politics. *Educational Evaluation and Policy Analysis, 9*(2), 85–100.

Boyd, W. L., & Hartman, W. T. (1987). The politics of educational productivity. In D. Monk & J. Underwood (Eds.), *Microlevel School Finance* (pp. 271–308). Cambridge, MA: Ballinger.

Business and Industry Association of New Hampshire. (1988). *An agenda for continued economic opportunity.* Accessed November 28, 1998, from www.jbartlett.org/mkt.html

Caldwell, B. J. (1989, March). *Paradox and uncertainty in the governance of education.* Paper presented at the annual meeting of the American Educational Research Association, San Francisco.

Campbell, R. F., Cunningham, L. L., Rystrand, R. O., & Usdan, M. D. (1975). *The organization and control of public schools.* Columbus, OH: Merrill.

Capodice, M., & Weld, J. (1989). *The marketplace heralds education reform.* Concord, NH: The Josiah Bartlett Center for Public Policy.

Carlson, R. O. (1964). Environmental constraints and organizational consequences: The public school and its clients. In D. E. Griffiths (Ed.), *Behavioral science and educational administration: The 63rd yearbook of the National Society for the Study of Education, Part II* (pp. 262–276). Chicago: National Society for the Study of Education.

Carnegie Forum on Education and the Economy. (1986, May). *A nation prepared: Teachers for the 21st century.* Washington, DC: Carnegie Forum on Education and the Economy.

Case, C. W. (1986, July, August). The Holmes group report: Impetus for gaining professional status for teachers. *Journal of Teacher Education, 37*(4), 36–44.

Charon, J. (1998). *Symbolic interactionism: An introduction, an interpretation, and integration.* Upper Saddle River, NJ: Prentice Hall.

Chubb, J. E. (1988, Winter). Why the current wave of school reform will fail. *Public Interest, 90*(Winter), 28–49.

Cobb, N. (1994). *The future of education: Perspectives on national standards in America.* New York: College Board.

Coffey, A., & Atkinson, P. (1996). *Making sense of qualitative data.* London: Sage.

Cogan, M. L. (1953). Toward a definition of profession. *Harvard Educational Reviews, 23*(1), 33–50.

Cohn, D., & Spillane, J. (1994). Policy and practice: The relations between governance and instruction. In N. Cobb (Ed.), *The future of education: Perspectives on national standards in America* (pp. 109–155). New York: College Board.

Cohn, M. M., & Kottkamp, R. B. (1993). *Teachers: The missing voice in education.* Albany: State University of New York Press.

Cohn, M. M., Kottkamp, R. B., & Provenzo, E. F., Jr. (1987). *To be a teacher: Cases, concepts, observation guides.* New York: Random House.

Coomb, F. S. (1987, April). *The effects of increased state control on local school district governance.* Paper presented at the annual meeting of the American Research Association, Washington, DC.

Cremin, L. A. (1961). *The transformation of the school.* New York: Alfred A. Knopf.

Cross, C. (1993, April 21). Education standards, a question of time. *Education Week.* Accessed March 30, 2004, from www.edweek.org

Cross, C. (1994). Implications of subject matter standards. In N. Cobb (Ed.), *The future of education: Perspectives on national standards* (pp. 43–50). New York: College Board.

Cuban, L. (1984). *How teachers taught: Constancy and change in American classrooms, 1890–1990.* New York: Longman.

Cuban, L. (1988). The fundamental puzzle of school reform. *Phi Delta Kappan, 69*(5), 340–344.

Cusick, P. A. (1992). *The educational system.* New York: McGraw-Hill.

Darling-Hammond, L. (1990, December). Achieving our goals: Superficial or structural reforms? *Phi Delta Kappan, 72*(4), 286–295.

Deci, E., & Ryan, M. (1982). Intrinsic motivation to teach: Possibility and obstacles in our colleges and universities. In J. L. Bess (Ed.), *New directions in teaching and learning* (pp. 27–35). San Francisco: Jossey-Bass.

Denzin, N. (1989). *Interpretive interactionism.* London: Sage.

Diegmueler, K. (1994). English group loses funding for standards. *Education Week,* 21–23. Accessed March 30, 2004, from www.edweek.org

Douglas, J. (1985). *Creative interviewing.* Beverly Hills, CA: Sage.

Doyle, D. P., & Hartle, T. W. (1985, September). Leadership in education: Governors, legislators and teachers. *Phi Beta Kappan, 67*(1), 21–27.

Dreeban, R. (1973). The school as a workplace. In R. M. W. Travers (Ed.), *Secondary handbook of research in teaching* (pp. 450–470). Chicago: Rand McNally.

Dreeban, R., & Barr, R. (1983). Educational policy and the working of schools. In L. S. Shulman & G. Sykes (Eds.), *Handbook of teaching and policy* (pp. 81–94). New York: Longman.

Eagleton, T. (1991). *Ideology: An introduction.* New York: Verso.

Editorial Projects in Education (1998, January 21). News: A Goals 2000 timeline. *Education Week.* Accessed January 12, 1998, from www.edweek.org

Education Commission of the States. (1983). *Action for excellence.* Denver, CO: Education Commission of the States.

Educational Testing Service. (1991). *The state of inequality.* Princeton, NJ: Educational Testing Service.

Educational Testing Service. (2002). *A national priority: Americans speak on teacher quality.* Accessed June 28, 2007, from www.ets.org

Elkind, D. (1989). Developmentally appropriate practice: Philosophical and practical applications. *Phi Delta Kappan, 71*(2), 113–117.

Elsbree, W. S. (1939). *The American teacher.* Glenview, IL: American Book Co.

Elwein, M. C., Glass, G. V., & Smith, M. L. (1988). Standards of competence: Propositions on the nature of testing reform. *Educational Researcher, 17*(8), 4–9.

Erickson, D. A. (1979, March). Research on educational administration: The state-of-the-art. *Educational Researcher, 8*(3), 9–14.

Evertson, C. (1985). Making a difference in education quality through teacher education. *Journal of Teacher Education, 36*(3), 2–12.

Feinberg, W. (1983). *Understanding education.* New York: Cambridge University Press.

Feinberg, W. (1985, Fall). Fixing the schools: The ideological turn. *Issues in Education, 3*(2), 113–138.

Feinberg, W. (1987). The Holmes Group report and the professionalization of teaching. *Teachers College Record, 88*(3), 336–377.

Ferguson, R. F. (1998). Teachers' perceptions and expectations and the black-white test score gap. In C. Jencks and M. Phillips (Eds.), *The black-white test score gap and can schools narrow the black-white test score gap?* (pp. 273–374). Washington, DC: Brookings Institution Press.

Ferguson, R. F., & Ladd, H. F. (1996). How and why Monday matters: An analysis of Alabama schools. In H. F. Ladd (Ed.), *Holding schools accountable: Performance-based reform education.* Washington, DC: Brookings Institution Press.

Figlio, D. (2002, February 13). *Aggregation and accountability: Will no child truly be left behind?* Washington, DC: Fordham Foundation.

Firestone, W. A. (1990). Continuity and incrementalism after all: State responses to the excellence movement. In J. Murphy (Ed.), *The educational reform movements of the 1980's: Perspectives and cases* (pp. 143–166). Berkeley, CA: Mc-Cutchan.

Foster, W. (1994). Toward a critical practice of leadership. In J. Smyth (Ed.), *Critical perspectives on educational leadership* (pp. 39–62). Philadelphia: Falmer Press.

Foucault, M. (1980). *Power/knowledge: Selected interviews and other writings, 1972–1977* (C. Gordon, Ed.). New York: Pantheon.

Freeman, D. J., Martin, R. J., Brousseau, B. A., & West, B. (1988, April). *Do higher program admission standards alter profiles of entering teacher candidates?* Paper presented at the annual meeting of the American Educational Research Association, New Orleans, LA.

Freire, P. (1996). *Pedagogy of the oppressed.* New York: Continuum.

Fuhrman, S. (1988). State politics and school reform. In R. Crowson & J. Hannaway (Eds.), *The politics of reforming school administration.* New York: Falmer Press.

Fuhrman, S., & Elmore, R. (1994). Educational proficiency and curriculum governance. The governance of curriculum. Yearbook. Alexandria, VA: Association for Supervision and Curriculum Development.

Gallup, A., & Elam, S. (1988). The twentieth annual Gallup poll of the public's attitudes towards public schools. *Phi Delta Kappan, 70*(1), 33–46.

Gallup, A., & Rose, L. (2005). The American public: More informed about NCLB and more skeptical about its strategies. *Phi Delta Kappa International.* Accessed August 23, 2007, from www.pdkintl.org

Gandal, M., & Vranek, J. (2001, September). Standards: Here today, here tomorrow. *Educational Leadership, 59*(1), 456–568.

Gilles, J., Gelleta, S., & Daniels, M. (1994, March). *What makes a good school? A methodological critique and reappraisal.* Paper presented at the annual meeting of the Midwest Sociological Society, St. Louis, MO.

Gillman, D., & Reynolds, R. (1991). The side effects of statewide testing. *Contemporary Education, 62*(4), 273–278.

Giroux, H. (1988). *Teachers as intellectuals: Toward a critical pedagogy of learning.* Granby, MA: Bergin & Garvey.

Glazer, N. (1974). The schools of the minor professions. *Minerva, 12*(3), 346–364.

Goode, W. J. (1962). The librarian: From occupation to profession? In P. H. Ennis & H. W. Winger (Eds.), *Seven questions about the profession of librarianship* (pp. 8–22). Chicago: University of Chicago Press.

Goodlad, J. I. (1984). *A place called school: Prospects for the future.* New York: McGraw-Hill.

Goodlad, J. I. (1991). *Teachers for our nation's schools.* San Francisco: Jossey-Bass.

Green, J. (1987). *The next wave: A synopsis of recent educational reform reports.* Denver, CO: Education Commission of the States.

Greene, M. (1978). *Landscapes of learning.* New York: Teachers College Press.

Greene, M. (1988). *The dialectic of freedom.* New York: Teachers College Press.

Guthrie, J. W. (1985). The education policy consequences of economic instability: The emerging political economy of American education. *Education Evaluation and Policy Analysis, 7*(4), 319–332.

Guthrie, J. W., & Kirst, M. W. (1988, March). *Conditions of education in California, 1988.* Policy Paper No. 88–3-2. Berkeley: Policy Analysis for California Education.

Haladyna, T. M., Nolan, S. B., & Hass, N. S. (1991). Raising standardized achievement test scores and the origins of test pollution. *Educational Researcher, 20*(5), 2–7.

Hawley, W. D. (1988, November). Missing pieces of the education reform agenda: Or why the first and second waves may miss the boat. *Education Administration Quarterly, 24*(4), 416–437.

Holmes Group. (1986). *Tomorrow's teachers.* East Lansing, MI: Holmes Group.

Honawar, V. (2007, April 27). Teachers of the year seek voice in NCLB rewrite. *Education Week.* Accessed August 28, 2007, from www:edweek.org

Huebner, D. (1966). Curricular language and classroom meaning. In J. Macdonald & R. Leeper (Eds.), *Language and meanings* (pp. 8–26). Washington, DC: Association for Supervision and Curriculum Development.

Jackson, P. (1968). *Life in classrooms.* New York: Holt, Rinehart & Winston.

Jacobson, L. (1998). Seizing the moment. *Education Week, 17*(17), 202–203.

Kirst, M. (1984, November). The changing balance in state and local power to control education. *Phi Beta Kappan, 66*(3), 189–191.

Kirst, M. (1987, October). PEER: An interview with Michael Kirst. *Phi Delta Kappan, 60*(2), 161–164.

Kirst, M., & Guthrie, J. (1994). Goals 2000 and a reauthorized ESEA: National standards and accompanying controversies. In N. Cobb (Ed.), *The future of education: Perspectives in national standards in America.* New York: College Board.

Koretz, D., Madaus, G., Haertel, E., & Beaton, A. (1992). *National education standards and testing: A response to the recommendations of the national council on education standards and testing.* Santa Monica, CA: Institute on Education and Training, The Rand Corporation.

Kozol, J. (1996). *On being a teacher.* Oxford, UK: Oneworld.

Lee, J. (2002). *Evaluating rural progress in mathematics achievement: Is adequate yearly progress (AYP) feasible, valid, reliable, and fair?* Paper prepared for the ACCLAIM conference, SUNY–Buffalo, 3–6 November.

Lewin, K. (1947). Frontiers in group dynamics: Concept, method and reality in social equilibria and social change. *Human Relations, 1*(1), 5–41.

Lieberman, A., & Miller, L. (1990). Teacher development in professional practice schools. *Teachers College Record, 92*(1), 105–122.

Lincoln, B. (1989). *Discourse and the construction of society: Comparative studies of myth, ritual, and classification.* New York: Oxford University Press.

Lortie, D. C. (1969). The balance of autonomy and control in elementary school teaching. In A. Etzioni (Ed.), *The semi-professions and their organization: Teachers, nurses, and social workers* (pp. 1–53). New York: Free Press.

Lortie, D. C. (1975). *Schoolteacher: A sociological study.* Chicago: University of Chicago Press.

Lortie, D. C. (1988). Built-in tendencies toward stabilizing the principal's role. *Journal of Research and Development in Education, 22*(1), 80–90.

Loveless, T. (1994). The politics of national standards. In N. Cobb (Ed.), *The future of education: Perspectives on national standards in America.* New York: College Board.

Lukes, S. (1974). *Power: A radical view.* London: Macmillan.

Lyotard, J. F. (1984). *The postmodern condition: A report on knowledge.* Manchester, UK: Manchester University Press.

Madaus, G. F. (1989). New ways of thinking about testing: An interview with George Madaus. *Phi Delta Kappan, 70*(8), 642–645.

Madaus, G. F., & Pullin, D. (1987). Teacher certification tests: Do they really measure what we need to know? *Phi Delta Kappan, 69*(1), 31–38.

Marcoulides, G. A., & Heck, R. H. (1990). Educational political issues for the 1990's: Balancing equity and excellence in the implementation of the reform agenda. *Urban Education, 25*(1), 55–67.

Marshall, C., & Rossman, G. (1995). *Designing qualitative research.* Thousand Oaks, CA: Sage.

Mathis, W. (2003, May). No child left behind: Costs and benefits. *Phi Delta Kappan, 84*(9), 679–686.

McClellan, M. C. (1988, June). Testing and reform. *Phi Delta Kappan, 69*(10), 768–771.

McCloskey, G. N., Provenzo, E. F., Cohn, M. M., & Kottkamp, R. B. (1987). *A profession at risk: Legislated learning as a disincentive to teaching.* (Contract No. ERI-P-86–3088). Washington, DC: U.S. Department of Education, Office of Educational Research and Improvement. (ERIC Document Reproduction Service No. ED 284 844).

McNeil, L. M. (1986). *Contradictions of control: School structure and school knowledge.* New York: Routledge & Kegan Paul/Methuen.

McNeil, L. M. (1988). Contradictions of control, Part 3: Contradictions of reform. *Phi Delta Kappan, 69*(7), 478–485.

Mead, G. (1934). *Mind, self, and society.* Chicago: University of Chicago Press.

Messick, S. (1984). The psychology of educational measurement. *Journal of Educational Measurement, 21*(3), 215–237.

Meyer, J. W. (1977). Institutionalized organization: Formal structure as myth and ceremony. *American Journal of Sociology, 83*(2), 540–563.

Mitchell, D. E., & Encarnation, E. J. (1984, May). Alternative state policy mechanisms for influencing school performance. *Educational Researcher, 13*(5), 4–11.

Mitchell, D. E., & Keerchner, C. T. (1983). Labor relations and teacher policy. In L. S. Shulman & G. Sykes (Eds.), *Handbook of teaching and policy* (pp. 214–238). New York: Longman.

Monk, D. H. (1994). Subject matter preparation of secondary mathematics and science teachers and student achievement. *Economics of Education Review, 13*(2), 125–145.

Moore, W. (1970). *The professions: Roles and rules.* New York: Russell Sage Foundation.

Murphy, J. (1990). *The educational reform movement of the 1980's: Perspectives and cases.* Berkeley, CA: McCutchan.

Murray, S. L. (1986). *Considering policy options for testing teachers.* Contract No. 400–86–0006. Portland, Oregon: Northwest Regional Educational Library. (ERIC Document Reproduction Service No. ED 276 721).

Nader, R. (1987). Sixty years of idiocy is enough. *Fair Test Examiner, 1*(1), 1, 3.

National Board of Teaching Standards. (1994). *Statement of guiding principles.* Detroit, Michigan.

National Center for Education Statistics. (1997). *Digest of education statistics.* Washington, DC: U.S. Department of Education, Office of Education Research and Improvement. NCES98–015.

National Center for Education Statistics. (2002). *Digest of educational statistics.* Washington, DC: U.S. Department of Education, Office of Education Research and Improvement. Accessed August 28, 2007, from www.ed.gov

National Commission on Excellence in Education. (1983). *A nation at risk: The imperative of educational reform.* Washington, DC: U.S. Government Printing Office.

National Commission on Testing and Public Policy. (1990). *From gatekeeper to gateway: Transforming testing in America.* Chestnut Hill, MA: Boston College.

National Council on Education Standards and Testing. (1993). *Raising standards for American education.* Washington, DC: National Education Goals Panel.

National Education Association. (1992). *Status of the American public school teacher, 1990–1991.* Washington, DC: National Education Association Research Division.

National Education Commission on Time and Learning. (1994). *Prisoners of time: Research on what we know and what we need to know.* Washington, DC: U.S. Government Printing Office.

National Education Goals Panel. (1996). *A report of the goal 4 resource group on teacher education and professional development.* Washington, DC: U.S. Department of Education Publications.

National Governors' Association. (1986). *Time for results.* Washington, DC: Carnegie Forum on Education and the Economy.

National Science Board. (1983). *Educating Americans for the 21st century.* Washington, DC: National Science Board.

New Hampshire Department of Education. (1989). *State education improvement and assessment program.* Concord, NH: New Hampshire Department of Education.

New Hampshire Department of Education. (1996). *Report of governor's education summit.* Accessed October 14, 1998, from www.state.nh.us/governor/summit/p.2.html

New Hampshire Department of Education. (1997). *Questions and answers about the New Hampshire education improvement and assessment program (NHEIAP).* Concord, NH: New Hampshire Department of Education.

New Hampshire Department of Education. (1998a). *Local education improvement and assessment plan: Assistance program.* Concord, NH: New Hampshire Department of Education.

New Hampshire Department of Education. (1998b, February). *Report: Governor's task force on education adequacy.* Concord, NH: New Hampshire Department of Education.

New Hampshire Employment Security. (1987). *New Hampshire employment projections by industry and occupation.* Concord, NH: Economic and Labor Market Information Bureau.

New Hampshire Employment Security. (1997). *Vital signs: Economic indicators for New Hampshire.* Concord, NH: Economic and Labor Market Information Bureau.

New Hampshire State Government. (1993). *Title 15 education chapter 193-C: Statewide education improvement and assessment program.* Accessed March 30, 2004, from http://199.92.250.14/rsa/T15/C193-C/500003.html

New Hampshire State Government. (1997). *State of New Hampshire manual for the general court, 1997.* Concord, NH: New Hampshire State Government.

Nicoll, D. (1986). Leadership and followership. In J. Adams (Ed.), *Transforming leadership: From vision to results.* Alexandria, VA: Miles River Press.

Noyce, P. (2006, September 13). Professional development: How do we know if it works? *Education Week, 26*(3), 36–44.

Olson, L. (1988). Reform: Plaudits for staying power, prescriptions for new directions. *Education Week, 7*(32), 20–21.

Olson, L. (1989, 22 February). Governors say investment in children can curb "long-term costs" for states. *Education Week, 8*(22), 10.

Olson, L. (2001). Usefulness of annual testing varies by state. *Education Week.* Accessed February 21, 2007, from www.edweek.org

Orrill, R. (1994). Titanic structure on human scale: School reform at the close of the twentieth century. In N. Cobb (Ed.), *The future of education: Perspectives on national standards in America* (pp. 3–16). New York: College Board.

Osterman, K., & Kottkamp, R. (1993). *Reflective practice for educators: Improving schooling through professional development.* Newbury Park, CA: Corwin Press.

Parsons, T. (1968). Professions. In D. L. Sills (Ed.), *International encyclopedia of the social sciences, Vol. 12* (pp. 536–547). New York: Macmillan and Free Press.

Passow, A. H. (1984). Tackling the reform reports of the 1980's. *Phi Delta Kappan, 65*(10), 674–683.

Pearson, B. (1994, March 30). English group loses funding for standards. *Education Week,* 21–23. Accessed September 24, 1994, from www.edweek.org

Podham, W. J. (1985). Recertification test for teachers. *Educational Measurement: Issues and Practice, 4*(3), 23–25.

Popkewitz, T. (1982). *The myth of education reform.* Madison: University of Wisconsin Press.

Porter, A. C. (1988, April). *External standards and good teaching: The pros and cons of telling teachers what to do.* Paper presented at the annual meeting of the American Research Association, New Orleans, LA.

Public Agenda. (2001). Reality Check. *Public Agenda Online.* Accessed August 28, 2007, from www.publicagenda.org/specials/rc2001

Rose, L., & Gallup, A. (2002). The 34th annual phi delta kappa/gallup poll of the public's attitudes toward public schools. *Phi Delta Kappan, 84*(1), 41–56.

Rosenholtz, S. (1989). *Teachers' workplace: The social organization of schools.* New York: Longman.

Roth, R., & Pipho, C. (1990). Teacher education standards. In W. Houston (Ed.), *Handbook on teacher education* (pp. 119–135). New York: Macmillan.

Sanders, W., & Rivers, J. (1996). *Cumulative and residual effects of teachers on future student academic achievement.* Knoxville: University of Tennessee Value-Added Research and Assessment Center.

Sarason, S. B. (1990). *The predictable future of educational reform: Can we change course before it is too late?* San Francisco: Jossey-Bass.

Schaefer, R. (1967). *The school as a center of inquiry.* New York: Harper & Row.

Schon, D. A. (1987). *Educating the reflective practitioner.* San Francisco: Jossey-Bass.

Schouten, F. (2003). *School exit exams wreak havoc.* Ganett News Service. Accessed August 28, 2007, from www.defnews.com/2003/schools

Sedlack, M. C., Wheeler, C. W., Pullin, D. C., & Cusick, P. A. (1986). *Selling students short: Classroom bargains and academic reform in the American high school.* New York: Teachers College Press.

Smith, B. (2000, December). Quantity matters: Annual instruction time in an urban school system. *Educational Administration Quarterly, 36*(5), 652–682.

Smith, M. L. (1991). Put to the test: The effects of external testing on teachers. *Educational Researcher, 20*(5), 8–11.

Smith, M. L., Prunty, J. J., Dwyer, D. C., & Kline, P. F. (1987). *The fate of the innovative school: The history and present status of the Kensington School.* New York: Falmer Press.

Smyth, J. (1989). *Critical perspectives on educational leadership.* Philadelphia: Falmer Press.

Sommerfield, M. (1996, May 22). *New Hampshire governor uses veto to reject Goals 2000 money. Education Week.* Accessed March 30, 2004, from www.ed/week.org/ew/vol-15/35nh

Star, P. (1982). *The social transformation of American medicine.* New York: Alfred A. Knopf.

Stinchcombe, A. L. (1965). Social structures and organizations. In J. G. March (Ed.), *Handbook of organizations* (pp. 142–193). Chicago: Rand McNally.

Taylor S., & Bogdan, R. (1984). *Introduction to qualitative research: The search for meanings* (2nd ed.). New York: John Wiley.

Twentieth Century Fund. (1983). *Making the grade.* New York: Twentieth Century Fund.

Tyack, D. B. (1967). *Turning points in American education history.* Waltham, MA: Blaisdell.

Tyack, D. B. (1974). *The one best system: A history of American urban education.* Cambridge, MA: Harvard University Press.

Tyack, D. B. (1990). "Restructuring" in historical perspective: Tinkering toward utopia. *Teachers College Record, 92*(2), 170–191.

Tyack, D. B., & Cuban, L. (1995). *Tinkering toward utopia: A century of public school reform.* Cambridge, MA: Harvard University Press.

Underwood, J. (1989). State legislative responses to educational reform literature. In L. S. Lotto and P. W. Thurston (Eds.), *Recent advances in educational administration, Vol. 1.* Greenwich, CT: JAI Press.

U.S. Department of Education. (1989). *National education goals.* Washington, DC: U.S. Department of Education.

U.S. Department of Education. (1991a). *America 2000: An education strategy.* Washington, DC: U.S. Department of Education.

U.S. Department of Education. (1991b). *America 2000: A sourcebook.* Washington, DC: U.S. Department of Education.

U.S. Department of Education. (1993). *Improving America's schools act—1993.* Washington, DC: U.S. Department of Education.

U.S. Department of Education. (1994). *National education goals.* Washington, DC: U.S. Department of Education.

U.S. Department of Education. (1996). *Using federal resources to support reform.* Washington, DC: U.S. Department of Education.

U.S. Department of Education. (2002). *Strategic plan 2002–2007.* Washington, DC: U.S. Department of Education.

Usher, R., & Edwards, R. (1994). *Postmodernism and education.* New York: Routledge.

Viadero, D. (2003). Researchers debate impact of test. *Education Week.* Accessed February 5, 2007, from www.edweek.org

Willower, D. J. (1977). Schools and pupil control. In D.A. Erickson (Ed.), *Educational organization and administration* (pp. 296–310). Berkeley, CA: McCutchan.

Willower, D. J., Eidell, T. L., & Hoy, W. K. (1973). *The school and pupil control ideology (University Park PA: Pennsylvania State University Studies, No. 24)* (2nd ed.). University Park, PA: Pennsylvania State University.

Wirth, A. G. (1983). *Productive work in industry and schools: Becoming persons again.* Lanham, MD: University Press of America.

Wirth, A. G. (1992). *Education and the work for the year 2000: Choices we face.* San Francisco: Jossey-Bass.

Wise, A. E. (1979). *Legislated learning: The bureaucratization of the American classroom.* Berkeley and Los Angeles: University of California Press.

Wolf, D. (1994). Curriculum and assessment standards: Common measures or conversations? In N. Cobb (Ed.), *The future of education: Perspectives on national standards in America* (pp. 85–108). New York: College Board.

Young, M. (1971). *Knowledge and control.* London: Collier-Macmillan.

About the Author

Penny Ann Armstrong has been an educator for 25 years. She received her graduate degrees from the University of St. Thomas in Minneapolis, Minnesota, and has worked as a school administrator in Minnesota, New Hampshire, and Texas. Armstrong is the president of the Southwest Christian School and an instructor for Texas Wesleyan University in Fort Worth, Texas. In the summer of 2007, she was selected to be part of the Chinese government–sponsored Haliban Delegation of Educators to tour education facilities in Beijing. She is also the mother of four very smart people who have been the recipients of the experience of a generation of dedicated teachers.